TOWN GARDENS

TOWN GARDENS

CAROLINE BOISSET

LITTLE, BROWN AND COMPANY · BOSTON TORONTO LONDON

FIRST U.S. EDITION

Conceived, edited, and designed by Frances Lincoln Limited,
Apollo Works, 5 Charlton Kings Road, London NW5 2SB

Library of Congress Catalog Card Number 89-45828

10   9   8   7   6   5   4   3   2   1

Published simultaneously in Canada
by Little, Brown & Company (Canada) Limited
PRINTED IN HONG KONG
BY KWONG FAT OFFSET PRINTING CO., LTD.

CONTENTS

INTRODUCTION

Each city has its underlying style. The rock of the Acropolis was the Athenians' focus for contact with the higher powers. In Venice the sea which brought her wealth laps palace and cathedral and the city's square . . . Bruges, London, New York are revealing human landscapes, each in turn picturing the lives and aspirations of her citizens . . . As London and Paris are differing worlds, so are their gardens.

(Russell Page, *The Education of a Gardener*, London, 1962)

In the cities and towns of the world distinctive garden styles have evolved over the centuries, directed by the way of life of the people and their architecture, as well as by the regional climate and soil. In his *Education of a Gardener* the great garden designer Russell Page speaks of 'the Londoner who tries to create an air of the country', the Parisian 'forming flowers and trees into the decorative elements of an outdoor salon', of roof gardens topping the high buildings of New York, and of hilly Rome where 'the flowery roof-top of one house is often the garden or terrace of the one above'. The modern gardener can learn much about design from an understanding of some of the reasons, and historic fashions, that have influenced the shape of town gardens.

In springtime in southern Spain, the ancient city of Cordoba comes alight with flowers. Flower pots stand behind the wrought-iron grilles of the ground floor windows and on the balconies of the upper storeys, and are fixed to the walls of the buildings; roses, geraniums and plumbago cascade down, and the air is filled with perfume from the blossom of the orange trees that line the streets. The sight is dazzling, the atmosphere sweet with scent.

Cordoba stands at the junction between Muslim and Christian faiths, and gave to Christian Europe the Islamic concept of the enclosed garden. During the spring flower festival, the *Fiesta de los Patios*, the owners of some of the older houses in the town traditionally open their flower-filled courtyards to the public. The gardens that can then be seen have a distinctively Spanish style. Some display great elegance, in the way materials are associated, in the use of colour and of garden ornaments, and particularly in the plants – always, it seems, kept in perfect condition.

The courtyard must be among the oldest forms of garden designed by man. We know that ancient Egyptians, Persians and Greeks gathered as families in courtyards surrounded on all four sides by the house, and we can speculate on how they may have adorned and planted these outdoor rooms. However, the oldest courtyard gardens of which we have detailed knowledge are the Roman peristyles. From excavations, frescoes and contemporary writings we know that the focal point of the Roman garden was usually an altar, for the worship of the gods,

Left This courtyard garden in the Palacio de las Dueñas in Seville displays many historical influences, all adapted to a distinctively Spanish style. Richly planted beds separated by tiled paths are arranged in the basic pattern of the *chahar bagh*, the fourfold garden, handed down, through the Moors, from the ancient Persians. In the centre is a raised fountain surrounded by a bed of arum lilies. The colonnade, which provides a sheltered way between the different parts of the house, recalls the peristyle of Greek and Roman courtyard gardens.

Above On the rooftops of the Rockefeller Center, high above New York City, are the famous roof gardens laid out in the early 1930s by the English designer Ralph Hancock. Several distinct gardens have recently been restored. Here, box-edged beds of day lilies, pelargoniums and *Sedum telephium* surround an immaculate lawn.

but that the family would also eat (at masonry tables), entertain, play, and even keep pets in their gardens. Porticoes on one, two, three or all four sides of the peristyle provided a comfortable means of communication between the different quarters of the house, and Roman gardeners would grow plants up the columns.

Early gardens, of around the second century BC, were of an informal character, with large trees and shrubs which required little water – the only water available being that gathered from the roof into a large cistern. In one house, excavated in 1973, there is evidence of trees (probably fruit) grown as espaliers.

Later gardens, designed after the advent of the aqueduct, were more formal in style and relied heavily on large supplies of water. From Roman writers, especially Virgil and later Pliny, we know that the plantings were mainly of evergreens such as box, bay, myrtle, oleander and rosemary, with seasonal colour from violets, daisies, viburnums, lilies, roses, opium poppies and chrysanthemums. Small statues among the plants represented deities, cupids, animals or theatrical subjects. They were made most commonly of white marble, sometimes of bronze or coloured marble. There were also sundials, terms capped with sculpted busts, rectangular reliefs with carvings on both sides, and many carved decorations that were hung on walls or between the columns of the porticoes.

As skill in water engineering increased, pools and fountains were introduced into gardens. Examples of peristyles constructed as pools, with raised brick ornamental beds, have recently been discovered; frescoes around their walls give a lush backdrop of greenery. Frescoes were often an integral part of the garden design, giving an illusion of depth and space to the small peristyle – and depicting, for those who could not have them, fountains, pools, trees, and, more ambitiously, lakes and mountains.

From the seventh and eighth centuries AD we have descriptions of courtyard gardens in towns of the Islamic civilization. The fundamental pattern followed in these gardens was that of the *chahar bagh*, the fourfold garden – a pattern that dates back to the earliest Persian gardens of 2000 BC, and has remained to this day the basis of gardens in the Persian tradition. The garden was divided into quarters, usually by four channels that met at a central focal point in the form of a pool, a fountain or a pavilion. The quarters signified the four elements of water, fire, air and earth.

In the parched lands of the Middle East, the key feature of the Islamic courtyard garden was water. Its potential was exploited to the maximum – the limits being set by availability, the size of the garden and the wealth of the owner. Pools were strictly geometrical and in the larger gardens were surrounded by symmetrically arranged channels, cascades and fountains that echoed each other visually and in sound. Pools were kept filled to capacity, and served not only the aesthetics of the enclosure but also as reservoirs to irrigate the plants. These plants were usually in narrow beds, less often in pots: gardens had trees such as pomegranates, olives, citrus and figs for fruit and shade, with flowers such as roses, lilies and tulips for colour and scent. The materials used were stone, marble, ceramic tiles, mosaic and painted wood, and courtyards were divided by fretted and carved wooden screens.

The concept of the enclosed garden was carried by the invading Moors as far as southern Spain. Later, influences from the Middle East were also spread throughout Europe by the Crusaders, who brought back with them new ideas and plants for the gardens that nestled within the walls of their castles, which were little towns in themselves. I know of three reconstructions of medieval gardens, all of them potential sources of inspiration to the town gardener. One has been re-created at the Cloisters, the medieval section of the Metropolitan Museum of Art in New York City, another is in the Château

Right The small Tudor knot garden at the Museum of Garden History of the Tradescant Trust, in London, was designed by the Marchioness of Salisbury, faithfully following a pattern of the period and using only plants known to have been in cultivation in the time of John Tradescant the Elder, gardener to the Salisbury family in the sixteenth century. The osier frames are designed to have plants trained over them.

Left The Cuxa Cloister, the largest of the three gardens at the Cloisters, the medieval section of the Metropolitan Museum of Art in New York, which were recently renovated following original plans. All the plants used are known to have been grown in medieval times, and many have been identified in paintings and tapestries in the museum's collection.

de Busseol high up in the Massif Central in France, and the third is in southern England, under the walls of the old castle in Winchester.

The focal point of a medieval castle garden might be a small fountain or channel with a lead-lined pool, or an arbour made of coppiced hazel or chestnut poles held together with willow, and with vines and roses growing over it. It was commonly surrounded by a lawn of wild flowers and beds of herbs and ornamental plants such as lilies, orris, heart's-ease, hellebores, wormwood, sage, rue, borage, soapwort, lavender, cornflowers, pot marigolds and peonies. Seats were of stone or wood, or of camomile or turf.

A little later gardens appeared in larger European towns, including London, Paris and Amsterdam. Most of these were utilitarian, with fruit trees, vegetables and herbs, and space for a few hens or ducks. However, and perhaps more relevant to the present-day town gardener, it is possible to find, in medieval illuminated manuscripts and Renaissance paintings, portrayals of balconies, window boxes and pots placed along the parapets of buildings – demonstration of a long tradition of growing plants in any tiny space available.

The sixteenth century saw the development of knot gardens, with ornamental garden beds laid out in a pattern of lines of low evergreen bushes, such as thyme, hyssop, box or wall germander, the gaps between being filled with flowers or herbs, or coloured materials such as sand or brick dust. The knot garden was the forerunner of the parterre, the regularly laid out formal flower garden that is still a key feature in garden design, and is particularly well suited to the town garden.

The meticulous restoration of the town of Williamsburg in Virginia has provided us with fine re-creations of some of the small town gardens of early eighteenth-century America. By colonial law each house was allotted a half-acre plot, and the garden became an integral part of the whole design, with the subsidiary buildings ranged round the sides, enclosing it and offering protection from the weather and intruders. In style the gardens followed the pattern the settlers had brought with them from seventeenth-century England.

Every effort has been made to ensure that the restored Williamsburg gardens are typical of the period, and only plants known to have been in cultivation in the United States before 1800 have been used. The hedging and topiary are mainly of box (*Buxus sempervirens* and its dwarf variety *B. sempervirens* 'Suffruticosa'), which withstands the extremes of temperature of inland Virginia, with its hot summer sun and winter frosts. Native American species used include elm, hemlock, the scarlet oak (*Quercus coccinea*), *Magnolia grandiflora*, dogwood (*Cornus florida*), redbud (*Cercis canadensis*), hollies, and the hardy bayberry (*Myrica pensylvanica*). Within the parterres and in flower beds are tulips in profusion, amidst pinks, hollyhocks, larkspur, foxgloves and roses – all introduced by way of England – and the American phlox, coreopsis and gaillardia.

In both Europe and the United States, town gardens as most of us know them today – those awkwardly shaped strips of land behind rows of houses – really only came into existence in the mid-eighteenth century, with the increase in building to meet the needs of the rapidly growing population. At first the space behind a small town house functioned only as a utilitarian back yard, the site for such commodities as the privy and the washing line. But during the second half of the century, in England and Holland, the back garden began to be considered as a visual adjunct to the house. The standard design, which was to persist into the middle of the nineteenth century, was a geometric pattern edged with box, usually set in gravel, with stone slab paths down either side for comfortable access. Some of these gardens held interesting collections of plants, including new introductions from overseas.

One such garden, the London garden of Francis Douce, Keeper of Manuscripts at the British Museum, is well documented in correspondence with Richard Twiss, who supplied the plan in 1781. The basic design was simple enough, respecting the rules of symmetry and formality that were all-important at the period. There was a hedge of poplars around the whole garden with, inside it, a wide gravel walk surrounding a large central bed edged in box. The planting outlined on the plan was mainly of a mixture of evergreen and deciduous shrubs, many of them introductions from North America. They included *Kalmia, Robinia hispida, Colutea, Arbutus unedo, Cistus ladanifer, Hibiscus syriacus*, the evergreen *Phillyrea*, laurustinus (*Viburnum tinus*), an azalea and some roses for scent, two double-flowering cherries and, in the centre, an almond (which was an afterthought replacing an earlier suggestion for a tulip tree, *Liriodendron tulipifera*). At the far end of the

Top In the restored eighteenth-century gardens of Colonial Williamsburg, periwinkle and ivy supply permanent ground cover within the box-edges parterres, while an interplanting of bulbs brings colour in spring. Topiary specimens provide focal points, and trees such as elm and the scarlet oak offer shade in the hot Virginian summer.

Above The plan for the restored Orlando Jones garden at Williamsburg. The oval pleasure garden is surrounded by box hedging and divided into two symmetrical beds that are filled with daisies (*Bellis perennis*) and white lily-flowered tulips in winter and spring and in the summer with globe amaranth (*Gomphrena globosa*). In the centre is a paper mulberry tree (*Broussonetia papyrifera*) surrounded by orange day lilies. Benches at the four corners of the garden are shaded by crape myrtle trees (*Lagerstroemia indica*).

garden the gravel path opened up into a semicircle in which was positioned a bench flanked by two evergreen *Rhododendron ponticum*. There was also a passion flower grown in a box, and in other pots there were auriculas and polyanthus.

In the early nineteenth century, under the Regency, the fashion for balconies reached its zenith in Britain, with covered balconies forming elegant adjuncts to otherwise simple terraced houses. Many terraces overlooked tree-planted squares; creating a garden on the balcony reinforced the country house illusion.

Somewhat later, and at a different social level, numerous worthy pamphlets were published advocating window box gardening as a means of improving the homes and environments of the poor. Catherine Buckton, author of *Town and Window Gardening*, 1879, reports that the children of Leeds cultivated pretty window boxes in cartons acquired from the local grocer.

As the century advanced, there came developments in technology that revolutionized town gardening. Probably most significant of all was the invention, in 1830, of the lawn mower – a machine that brought a tidy lawn within the reach of the middle-class gardener. Another innovation, of significance to many town gardeners, was marked at the Paris World Exhibition of 1867, where the German master builder Carl Rabbitz showed a plaster model of a roof garden on the flat roof of his Berlin house, which he had waterproofed using his own patented vulcanized cement.

The roof garden offers to town gardeners the inestimable advantage that it does not require any more land than the house itself; and in towns where the climate is mild and the rainfall low there have been small rooftop terraces decorated with potted plants at least since the ancient Greeks balanced pots on parapets. However, any rooftop planting of a more extensive nature requires a flat roof constructed to a very high standard, to avoid damage from water leakage. Until the technological advances of the late nineteenth and early twentieth centuries the prohibitive cost limited such planting to a very few buildings. Since then, roof gardens have been a feasible proposition even in countries with cold, wet winters.

Another feature of nineteenth-century life was a great increase in the dissemination of knowledge, with the widespread publication of books and periodicals. *Le Jardinier des Fenêtres, des Appartements et des Petits Jardins*, with information on how to grow fruit and flowers in tiny spaces in towns, was published in Paris in 1823 and remained popular throughout the century. In England, John Claudius Loudon, supported by his wife Jane, led the way. Together they encouraged their readers to plant both front and back gardens with a varied collection of shrubs and small trees. Resistance to town pollution (also increasing) was a prerequisite for plants, and emphasis was placed on keeping the maintenance bill to a minimum. The back garden was now regarded primarily as a place to walk in. The two lateral paths of the eighteenth century remained, but Loudon recommended planting a row of trees down the centre of the lawn, sufficiently far from the paths to avoid the necessity for an annual pruning of overhanging branches that would otherwise 'inconvenience persons passing along the walks'. He also advised against climbers that would 'incur the expense of training and pruning', ivy (gold, silver and common) being the only adornment for walls and fences. For the front garden he advocated planting one compact shrub, preferably an evergreen, in the centre of the lawn.

In the United States Andrew Jackson Downing adapted many of Loudon's theories to American conditions. Taking the landscape as his inspiration, and advocating a picturesque style more suited to the American taste, he also developed his own rules for garden design. He wanted every American to take pride in his garden, and insisted that even a single tree in a lawn surrounded by neat flower and shrub beds could be as beautiful as the large estates along the Hudson river. It was here that he had built his own home and designed his garden, a mixture of formal box-edged flower beds, gravel paths and sweeping lawns with the occasional specimen tree and arabesque beds for roses, geraniums and fuchsias. He also wrote an introduction to Jane Loudon's *Gardening for Ladies*, which was published in the United States in 1849 to encourage American women to take an active part in tending their gardens.

It was in the 1870s that the communicating front garden of the American small town made its appearance, as part of the idealistic dream of a perfect society living on what might appear to be communal land, as each plot was delineated from its neighbours only by unobtrusive markers.

In Europe, towards the end of the century, there came a period of stagnation in the development of town garden design. Probably the most significant factor in this was the growing problem of town pollution. The thick layers of soot deposited by factory chimneys poisoned much vegetation, greatly restricting the choice of plants. By the early years of the twentieth century probably the most common pattern for a small town garden consisted of a central patch of turf surrounded by a path, with a few narrow flower beds in the

In this small Dutch garden a geometric design is softened by informal planting. Trees and shrubs provide seclusion, and blur the garden's boundaries, making it seem larger than it really is. Beneath them perennials such as *Brunnera macrophylla*, geraniums and hellebores, interspersed with forget-me-nots, clothe the ground, and help suppress weeds. The quiet green of the lawn gives the garden a peaceful air, while the two clipped box balls at the end of the path add a touch of formality as they focus the attention and lead the eye across the lawn. Beyond cutting the grass and occasionally clipping the box, this garden needs little maintenance – an important consideration for a busy modern gardener.

shadiest part of the garden, against the wall. The garden would be maintained by the maid of the household and the owners might sit in it on sunny afternoons.

However, following the First World War there were several major changes that were to influence the development of town garden design. First, there were changes in life-style that gradually led to more use of the garden as extra living space. Hard, all-weather surfaces were increasingly popular, and garden furniture, to be used at every opportunity, became a design feature. Second was the emergence of abstract art, which passed into garden design in the form of hard shapes and asymmetrical spaces. This style is typified by the *art déco* gardens of the Palais Stoclet in Brussels, where stark gravel walks curve around tightly clipped topiary specimens against the clean lines of the palace.

In California, in the 1920s, the landscape architect Thomas Church began to evolve an attitude to garden design that has proved influential in the development of town gardens in the United States, in Europe, and in Australia. While Thomas Church regarded the garden as a work of art, he felt that the composition should arise from the requirements of the client

and the potential of the site. His approach was practical, and slanted towards outdoor living: he included in his garden designs space for eating, for playing, and wherever possible for swimming, and used large picture windows and glass sliding doors to bring the garden into the house. The atmosphere was relaxed and natural.

In the last thirty years, increases in prosperity and in leisure time have brought a surge of interest in gardens and gardening. In addition, the realization of how much land has been lost to urban development has fostered an interest in nature that has been translated, in gardening, into the ecological style: all over Europe and the United States there are movements that encourage people to allow grass to grow longer and to make efforts to attract wildlife to the garden – for example by constructing pools, or growing plants attractive to birds or butterflies. Laws that restrict pollution have made for cleaner air, and it is now possible to grow a wide variety of plants in towns. More recently there has been a movement in garden design to reinterpret historical styles with modern living in mind. And so today there is a wider choice than ever before, among both styles and plants for the town garden.

PLANNING AND DESIGNING

In town even more than in the country, a private
outdoor space is a precious luxury. Careful planning
will enable you to make the most of it. Before you even
begin to design, and certainly before deciding what to
plant, it is essential to consider how you would like to
use your town garden; you need to become familiar
with the characteristics of the site; and you will want to
give some thought to the style and atmosphere you
would like to create. Then you can begin to shape a
framework for your garden.

THE USE OF THE GARDEN

Russell Page wrote, in *The Education of a Gardener*, 'First of all, in the town as in the country, a wise garden designer will study his site in silence and consider carefully his clients, their taste, their wishes, their way of life, their likes and dislikes, and absorb all of these factors at least as important as the ground that lies in front of him . . .' This is sound advice for anyone embarking on a garden design. Think about what you want from your garden. Would you like an outdoor room, where you can relax and entertain? Perhaps you have children, who need space to play? At what times of the year, and of the day, will you be using the garden? There is little point in growing roses if you spend most of the summer away from home; and if you can only enjoy your garden in the evenings, it would be better to

grow tobacco plants, which give out their scent late in the day, than lewisias, which have flowers that are tightly closed by tea-time. Think, too, about the amount of time you will have, or can afford, to look after the garden.

In practice, of course, you will probably want your garden to serve several purposes; and its use will evolve and change with your life-style. But whatever your aim, and however simple or complex your garden, it should be a pleasure to look at from your house or apartment. There will probably be several view-points, especially if the garden is visible from different levels. At garden level, focal points in line with windows will give a feeling of space and depth. As the overall plan is viewed from higher up, detail dwindles and, if the impression is not to be

Far left Viewed either at ground level or from above, this simple, symmetrical garden layout is effective. The central paved path, framed by a pair of weeping willows, leads straight to the focal point of the white urn on its plinth. Different surfaces and variations in level help define separate areas of the garden.

Left The ground plan of 4 The Circus, Bath, displays the regard for simplicity and ease of maintenance that characterized eighteenth-century town gardens.

Right From inside the house looking out, there is only a glimpse of a building to serve as a reminder of the cityscape beyond the high garden walls. Carefully placed sculpture and clever planting draw the eye from the shady terrace by the house to the sunny lawn where forget-me-nots flower in spring, and on to the azaleas at the end of the garden.

indistinct, the garden must have a clear pattern. This can be very simple: dividing the garden into four with two crossing paths and a centrepiece will instantly impart a structure. We could all learn something about effective garden design from those eighteenth-century town gardens which were just parterres of box standing out boldly against a ground cover of gravel. The excavation of 4 The Circus, in Bath, revealed the exact pattern of the parterres, confirming the detail on contemporary plans. The design is simplicity itself: a central oval bed with two topiary specimens on either side and a circular bed at each end. These beds were almost certainly edged with box. Down the sides of the garden were flagstone paths, laid on ash and clinker, and there were long, narrow beds under the walls. Gravel was spread over the garden, in much the way that grass is used these days; it was little trouble to maintain, and could easily be raked over when it became black from the sooty atmosphere.

The view from a window can be framed by wall shrubs or climbers that have been carefully (or neglectfully) allowed to outgrow their allotted space. Plants should not be so overgrown that they block the light, or make window cleaning impossible; but it is a pity to keep them so neat that they are visible only from the outside looking towards the house, and not from the inside looking out. A few branches will brighten up the foreground of the view into the garden. *Chaenomeles, Kerria japonica, Clematis montana* and *Viburnum × juddii* flower in succession throughout the spring; *Cytisus scoparius, Philadelphus* 'Virginal', some of the large-flowered clematis and many climbing roses are good candidates for the summer months. Those that are fragrant will give additional pleasure in warm weather, when the windows are open.

Most of us hope to spend some time relaxing in our gardens: for me there is nothing more enjoyable than to sit in the garden in the cool of the evening, after a long working day, sipping a

refreshing drink, talking to friends or just listening to the sounds of the city winding down for the night. So I feel it is important to have adequate provision to sit out and entertain friends without the necessity for a major session of furniture removal, or a retrenchment into the house when daylight fails.

Garden seats need to be comfortable, attractive and weatherproof. If they are not comfortable no one will want to sit on them, and they might as well not be there; if they are unattractive they will mar the appearance of the garden; and if they are not weatherproof the effort of taking them in at the end of the day will be difficult to sustain and, left out, they will rapidly deteriorate. Iron furniture should be galvanized and painted, wood should be treated with a stain containing a preservative, or painted first with primer and then with good oil paint. Plastic furniture is trouble-free, and much of it is well made, sturdy and good value for money; but in my opinion it never looks as elegant as furniture in wood or iron. Wicker chairs have an old-fashioned charm, but unless you are prepared to go to the trouble of carrying them in and out, they are better reserved for use in the conservatory, or on a veranda.

PETER C. JONES

Above right Elaborate ironwork furniture complements the style of this elegant outdoor room, with its 'wall' of × *Cupressocyparis leylandii* and wooden decking 'floor'. The tall pink flowers and lush green foliage of the cleome framing the bench are echoed in the colouring of the cushions.

Right A white cast-iron seat in a secluded spot, framed by lilies, climbing roses, clematis and one of the weeping forms of the goat willow (*Salix caprea*), is an invitation to relax and enjoy the garden.

Left The slate-grey table, delicate ironwork chairs and grey-purple cushions that furnish this shady patio have been chosen to harmonize with the subdued colours of the brick paving and the surrounding plants.

The style of furniture you choose will depend on the style of the garden. Look for shapes that will give you lasting pleasure. There are interesting furniture designs by contemporary designers, and it is also worth seeking out furniture made by students or in country workshops. Antique period pieces are beyond the pockets of most of us, but good-quality reproductions are available. You may even be able to find someone prepared to reproduce for you a favourite design from the past, perhaps scaling it down, as most garden furniture was made for country gardens and is quite large.

Neutral colours are usually best for garden furniture. White is the most popular colour for ironwork, and black and shades of green are useful alternatives. While white stands out well against a dark green hedge, black looks good against a pale-coloured wall. Wooden furniture can be painted in the same colours, but stains are another possible choice: they give an interesting texture, and are available in several different colours, some of which can be combined to subtle effect. Colour contrast can be added with cushions and tablecloths – perhaps related to the colours of surrounding flowers.

Care is needed in positioning furniture. Sometimes a chair or table looks as if it is floating in the middle of the garden: you

Above left In a sheltered corner of this garden a substantial wooden bench stands flanked by Versailles *caisses*, with *Pyrus salicifolia* 'Pendula' and *Hydrangea petiolaris* to provide a leafy canopy in summer.

Left Painted a soft, sunny yellow, this simple folding furniture brings year-round colour to a shady basement courtyard. In the narrow beds around the edges, a mophead hydrangea glows white, and fern fronds, tall blue campanulas and the delicate yellow-green foliage of *Gleditsia triacanthos* 'Sunburst' are light and airy in effect. Fuchsias and pelargoniums in containers add colour in their season.

can avoid this problem by placing the furniture on an area of paving which relates to its overall shape, or partially screening it off to give the impression that it is in a separate room. A large single item, such as a bench, may serve to terminate an axis.

Garden lighting makes it possible to use the garden at night as well as in the daytime. Floods and other lamps provide overall lighting, spotlights can be used to accent points of interest, and lights such as flares and candles will create special effects. A water garden can be magically illuminated by specially sealed lamps that float, or are weighted down to sink.

Choose carefully where you want the light to fall. Some experimenting will probably be needed to find the best position for a lamp. The closer it is to a subject, the narrower the beam of light: a light at the base of a tree, shining up, will reveal the complex tracery of the foliage. For a tall or long wall several lights might be necessary, and the interaction of the beams will contribute an extra dimension of light and shade.

If you have children, you will certainly want to give them some thought when you are planning your garden. The great gardener Gertrude Jekyll was born in London, and her clearest memories of her early years in town were of gardens and green plants in Green Park and Berkeley Square. She recalls making daisy chains, the attraction of dandelions that her nurse would not allow her to take home to the nursery, and the smell of freshly cut grass. In a small garden paving provides a more hard-wearing play surface than a daisy-strewn lawn – which in wet weather can soon be reduced to a mud patch. Wide paths around flower beds can be a good solution to the problem of the conflicting needs of children and adults, giving a circuit for tricycles and an opportunity to teach children to respect plants.

In her book *Children and Gardens* Miss Jekyll writes at length about the importance of giving children their own individual little gardens. She is emphatic that a child's garden should be well sited and given every chance and help to succeed. There is nothing more demoralizing for a child than a barren patch in which just a few of the sprinkled seeds have germinated. It soon becomes weedy and unrewarding, and is then abandoned. She suggests a garden with narrow beds that little arms can reach from either side, surrounded by a small hedge of golden privet, which grows fast, is relatively cheap, and can be taken out when the child moves on to greater things. Annuals and bulbs will give encouraging results. For continuity, add a few flowering perennials, and, if there is space, a small shrub such as the lilac *Syringa meyeri* 'Palibin'. Salad vegetables and herbs are interesting too, and a simple parterre

In this city garden (featured on pages 86–7) different types of lighting are used with great skill. Carefully positioned spotlights, uplighters and floodlights draw the eye over the bridge to the summerhouse beyond. Lights show up the tracery of foliage and trelliswork and are reflected in both the water and the mirror under the bridge, creating a theatrical atmosphere.

spelling out the child's name in mustard and cress or colourful low-growing annuals is fun to achieve.

There is always an enormous choice of children's play apparatus on the market, but much of it is so large and bulky that it would dominate a small town garden. It is also quite expensive. For the money, I would rather see a small house or Noah's Ark made in stained or painted wood, or a swing with some tough climbers growing up the frame. But perhaps I am biased, as I have a romantic view of swings, and memories of spending hours on one as a child.

DESIGN LIMITATIONS

Once you have decided on the use you hope to get out of your garden, the next step is to identify its limitations. Town gardens tend to have particular constraints – many of which, once recognized as a challenge, can be turned to advantage.

When planning any garden, you will need to take into consideration such basic characteristics as climate and microclimate, sun and shade. As the air temperature of a city or large town

can be several degrees higher than that of the surrounding countryside, many urban gardens have an extremely favourable microclimate – which means that, with a little caring cultivation, luxuriant plant growth can be achieved. This is, of course, a great advantage, but it also has its drawbacks: plants can quickly outgrow their allotted space, and some thoughtful initial planning, and a good deal of pruning, may be needed to prevent the garden from becoming completely overgrown.

The amount of sun and shade, and when and where the light falls, largely depend on aspect. This again needs some attention when you are planning and planting your garden. For example, if you are to use your terrace for evening drinks, you will want to position it where the sun falls on summer evenings. And a plant that needs the conditions of a sunny border is unlikely to thrive in a shady aspect.

Because of the proximity of many buildings, and often of trees as well, shade is characteristic of town gardens. In hot, sunny countries shade is welcome: plants, like people, suffer in scorching direct sunlight. The Spanish patio garden and the courtyard gardens of the Middle East are designed to provide the maximum shade. In countries where sunshine is weaker and less abundant, shade does limit the choice of plants. Whether you live in a sunny country or one where the weather is often overcast, if your garden is shaded by buildings, or by trees on someone else's land, there is little alternative but to accept the situation and design around it. Even if the shade is cast by tall, dense trees in your own garden, my advice would be to work with the shady site, rather than fell the trees. Mature trees contribute so much to a townscape that every effort should be made to preserve them.

It is usually possible to modify the amount of shade cast by your own trees. A great deal can be achieved by pruning: often the canopy can be reduced by half without harming either the trees or the landscape. However, tree pruning is a skilled job, and it is wise to call in a professional tree surgeon, with the knowledge and experience, and (equally important) the equipment needed to complete the work safely.

Once a little light has been allowed into the garden, it is possible to grow an interesting collection of woodland plants. Many flower in spring, before the leaves create dense shade.

Right In the hot, sunny climate of Sydney, a house wall provides shade for tender *Cyathea* that in turn shade bird's nest ferns (*Asplenium nidus*) with their translucent, erect leaves and clivias (*Clivia miniata*) with floppy, strap-shaped foliage of a darker green. The contrasts between the different leaves are dramatically revealed in the play of light and shade. Hydrangeas, fuchsias and a choisya enjoy the stronger light that touches the edge of the retaining wall.

Left A bright collection of spring bulbs, planted in the shade of trees at the edge of this garden, brings a touch of the countryside to the town. Blue and white bluebells, jonquils, anemones and tulips flower before most trees are in full leaf.

Snowdrops, aconites, daffodils, bluebells, violets, lily of the valley and primroses all thrive in partial shade, and so do many good shrubs, including camellias, viburnums, hamamelis, pieris and some rhododendrons. During the summer months carpets of leaves – ivies, hostas, hellebores, epimediums, pachysandra and butcher's broom – will provide a lush background to the flowers of foxgloves, some lilies, trilliums and the spectacular *Cardiocrinum giganteum*.

Where it is not possible to modify deep shade, the most satisfactory solution is usually an architectural treatment of the space. With good-quality paving, and perhaps some sculpture and a mural on one of the walls, a small walled town garden can make a charming courtyard. Try to identify the best times and spots for light, and grow plants suited to the conditions. A collection of ivies and ferns can be grown among tufa and rocks; baskets of impatiens, hung on the walls at a height where there is more light, will provide a stunning display from above; trailing plants growing in troughs fixed high up on the walls will make a textured curtain.

Right Trellis screens that support a wealth of pot-grown climbing plants obscure the view into the seating area of a rooftop terrace, providing a degree of privacy. The white bridge links this area of the roof garden with the next.

Left In this heavily shaded little courtyard garden the architectural details are as important as the planting. It is almost entirely paved, with beautiful old flagstones and bricks laid in a pleasing pattern, and has a statue as its focal point. All the plants are shade-loving: there are hellebores, tiarellas and astrantia in raised beds and a hosta in a terracotta pot; the white-tipped leaves of *Fatsia japonica* 'Variegata' bring some contrasting light, while a pink geranium adds colour.

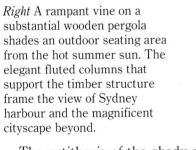

Right A rampant vine on a substantial wooden pergola shades an outdoor seating area from the hot summer sun. The elegant fluted columns that support the timber structure frame the view of Sydney harbour and the magnificent cityscape beyond.

The antithesis of the shady enclosed garden is the garden that is too exposed – physically to sun or wind, or (a particular problem for the town-dweller) visually to neighbours or passers-by. What is needed here is screening: this can take the form of a wall, trellis or fencing, a garden structure such as a pergola or an arbour, or tall or low plants, either clipped to make a formal hedge or left to grow informally. Which you choose will depend both on your specific purpose, or purposes, and on the style of your garden. Where the problem is too much sun, an overhead timber framework supporting some climbing plants is often a good solution: a well-positioned pergola will give shade from the hot summer sun, without blocking the low light of winter. A permeable barrier such as a hedge, a pergola or trellis provides protection from wind, while a wall just increases air turbulence. Only a solid barrier guarantees privacy, but a hedge, an open fence or a trellis with climbing plants is usually effective in obscuring the view into a garden, while still allowing light and air to penetrate.

In a sun-baked roof garden, designed by Isabelle Green, the patterns and textures of differently coloured gravels and of smooth sculptural stones contrast with spiky foliage plants and the twisting stems of a bougainvillea. The bougainvillea's strident, papery flowers dominate this austere garden during the hot summer months.

In this corner of a little roof garden, designed by Camille Muller, a wooden 'bridge' creates a change in level. Evergreen planting, in raised beds, ensures that the garden has interest throughout the year.

This tiny outdoor room, flanked on two sides by the roofs of adjoining buildings, is quite private and secluded. Plants in boxes along the parapet above the door, and in pots placed high above the seating area, cascade downwards. Since all the planting is in containers each plant can be given the type of soil it prefers, and here clematis and climbing roses, which prefer slightly alkaline conditions, thrive alongside acid-loving rhododendrons.

Roof gardens are almost always windswept, frequently sunbaked, and often open to onlookers from above. Screening materials for a roof garden must be selected with particular care, as they need to be light, to minimize the total load, as well as strong enough to withstand high-velocity winds. Here again a wooden pergola or a trellis arbour often provides the answer. Hardy climbers that can be grown in containers are best for clothing rooftop structures. I once grew a grape vine over a trellis arch on a town roof. I fed the vine copiously during the growing season, cut it back hard each winter and repotted it every two years, and it did very well. The herbaceous golden variegated hop, *Humulus lupulus* 'Aureus', is another vigorous climber that is good for rooftop screening.

Poor soil is common in town gardens, but this is less of a problem than it may at first seem. Even soil that appears irremediably spent, is thin and powdery or excessively heavy and full of builder's rubble, can be improved, if at a cost. New topsoil (or leafmould or well-rotted manure, if either is to be had) will improve both the structure and the nutritional content of the existing medium. The major advantage of importing new soil is that, to a great extent, it can be suited to the type of plant you wish to grow: peat increases the acidity of the soil; a quantity of limestone gravel increases alkalinity and improves drainage. A slow-release fertilizer mixed in with the soil when planting will ensure that a plant has a regular quantity of nutrients throughout the growing season. You can sprinkle pellets around the bases of the plants each year, to top up the supply.

The amount of water that plants need is almost always underestimated. Even in a generally mild, damp climate, additional watering is usually needed during the growing season. Try at the outset to make provision for a tap that is suitably positioned, preferably outside, to which you can attach a hose if necessary. This will not only be invaluable for watering, it will also make it possible to clean hard surfaces regularly: town gardens get very dirty. In hot countries washing down the paving will also cool the atmosphere.

Remember that access to most town gardens is through the house. To reach a roof garden you will have to go up stairs at best, up a ladder and over a parapet at worst. Bags of soil must be brought in, bags of leaves, prunings and other rubbish must be taken out. Avoid ordering large trees and shrubs that you cannot get to the garden without wrecking decoration and furniture on your way. Start with small specimens which, given adequate watering and feeding, in the warm microclimate of a town garden will soon grow to fill their space.

Pots and containers are useful additions to any garden, and in a small town garden, particularly one where conditions are less than ideal, they are invaluable. A patio, courtyard or roof garden, where the soil is either sparse or mostly covered in paving, will have most of its plants in containers. Here we can turn to Spain for inspiration and guidance. Spanish gardeners grow a lot of their plants in containers, tending them to perfec-

tion in the long, hot summers. They use pots to outline and punctuate pools, stand them on stairways, hang them on balconies and fasten them to walls around doors and windows. The plants they choose are often evergreen and, wherever possible, fragrant: rosemary, jasmine, wormwood, violets, oranges, box, myrtle, bay, oleander, almonds, hyacinths, jonquils, stocks, lilies and cyclamen are favourites. In colder climates *Viburnum × juddii* can be substituted for oleander, and apples for oranges.

The Spanish use lovely terracotta pots – most of them hand thrown, so each is slightly different from the next – and colourful glazed pots in green, yellow or blue. Beautiful traditional Chinese pots can also now be found in most parts of the world. Be careful, though, not to leave pots you treasure outside during the winter. Even pots that are supposed to be frost-resistant can be damaged if wet soil inside them freezes.

Left In this irregularly shaped courtyard garden, all the plants are contained in pots, and all have flowers of white or palest pink, to bring light to the shady setting. Hydrangeas and pelargoniums, which adapt themselves to the style of any garden, look appropriately formal in this outdoor room.

Right A mass of pots, most of them containing impatiens or ornamental grasses, almost covers the wooden decking of this tiny shaded garden. A few taller trees and shrubs, including a willow, *Salix matsudana* 'Tortuosa', add height, and the wooden arch that frames the door supports a honeysuckle and other climbing plants.

Stone troughs and urns give substance to a design. Cement and concrete are more commonly used these days, particularly for reproduction items, which often look very decorative. Containers made of lighter materials, such as plastic or expanded polystyrene, are easier to move around, but rarely attractive; you can camouflage them in *cache-pots*, or, alternatively, paint them black, stone colour or green.

Wood is another possible material. Versailles *caisses* can be as large as you want, and on wheels for ease of movement; and some are made, as the original ones were, so that they can be dismantled to allow the soil around the plants to be renewed. Half-barrels are a popular alternative, and they are traditional containers, but I always think they look rather incongruous in a garden.

Raised beds are often constructed on terraces, to provide space for more permanent plantings. They are larger than even the largest pots, and the soil they contain is in direct contact with the ground, providing opportunities for the roots to go deeper to find moisture. However, the soil they are on is likely to be packed with building rubble and other rubbish, and in this

Below left A timber Versailles *caisse* serves as an elegant raised bed in this narrow walled garden at the side of a town house. It is planted with a variegated holly for winter interest, and tall cornflowers, tumbling *Felicia amelloides* and small chrysanthemums for summer luxuriance. Nearby, two standard roses and a honeysuckle add interest to the white wall.

Below Decorated terracotta pots, planted with pelargoniums, petunias and trailing lobelia, make an eye-catching window display. The rounded foliage of phytolacca, azaleas and begonias in pots on the ground serves as a foil to the narrow leaves of irises behind the low front wall.

case, as with other container-grown plants, all nutrients will have to come from imported growing medium.

In the confined space of a town, many a garden consists solely of a window box, or boxes. There are many different types and styles of window boxes on the market, in materials from functional plastic to beautifully decorated terracotta. I generally prefer boxes made of traditional materials, with some aplomb. At one time a large part of my garden was contained in plain wooden boxes; I followed Gertrude Jekyll's advice and painted them black, which showed off plants to perfection. When you choose boxes, do take into consideration, not only the materials of your outer walls, but also the furnishings and decoration of the room behind. You should bear this in mind when you plant the boxes, too. One summer I opted for a traditional red, white and blue display of salvias, lobelia and alyssum. Viewed in isolation they looked spectacular, the alyssum frothing over and the lobelia cascading down. Unfortunately, against the old-gold curtains of my sitting room the effect was less satisfying. The following summer's sober array of purple Swiss balcony geraniums was much more successful.

Above right A weathered white wall and a dark evergreen myrtle provide an attractive background to a collection of terracotta pots. The larger containers are planted with rosemary and pale-leaved ballota, while the smaller ones hold pelargoniums, impatiens and lobelia.

Right A handsome terracotta pot with traditional incised decoration graces the corner of a terrace. The pot is permanently planted with an evergreen *Pittosporum tobira*, which is underplanted with alyssum in the summer months.

In a garden as tiny as a window box it is quite a challenge always to have something of interest growing, whatever the season. Evergreens such as trailing small-leaved ivies and miniature conifers provide a lasting framework, though they need renewing from time to time. A display of *Iris histrioides* 'Major' with a white crocus such as 'Snow Bunting' is fresh and pretty in earliest spring. After that, daffodils will carry you through for quite a time: you could perhaps try the early 'Beryl', followed by mid-season 'Professor Einstein', then the later-flowering 'Thalia'. The shorter-stemmed varieties are better adapted to the windy conditions of a window sill. Another spring choice might be white *Tulipa fosteriana* 'Purissima' with blue *Muscari armeniacum*. On a kitchen window sill, you could have herbs all through the summer, to be garnered for cooking as they are needed. Or, in a sunny position, you might like pelargoniums, which will flower through the summer, or petunias, which will last till the first frost. Neither pelargoniums nor petunias will tolerate deep shade, but impatiens is accommodating, and a white cultivar will bring a touch of light. Then if you plant pansies in late autumn they will begin to flower towards the end of the winter – earlier, if conditions are mild.

To produce a lasting display, you may need to do quite a bit of juggling. I had two identical sets of my wooden boxes, which I used to swap around. But fully planted boxes can be heavy, and you might not be able to lift them. An alternative solution is to have several plastic liners for each box: you can lift out the liner, with earth and plants, reline the box and start again.

The art of growing plants in containers lies in keeping the plants vigorous and in good condition, without doing so well that they become too big for their containers within the season. Always use good-quality potting compost and add a slow-release fertilizer at planting time and at the beginning of each growing season. Additional feeds of a liquid or soil fertilizer should be given to shrubs and small trees during the height of the growing season; stop feeding when it is time for the wood to mature in readiness for the winter. Annuals benefit from continual feeding until the end of the summer.

Left Tender plants thrive in containers in a conservatory. The pale complementary colours of yellow abutilon and blue *Plumbago auriculata*, twining together as they climb the wall, enhance the light, fresh atmosphere of this garden room (featured on pages 114–15). Other pots hold philodendron, basil, pelargoniums and many plants of fragrant white *Lilium regale*.

Plants in containers need a great deal of water. During a dry spell in summer this may mean daily or even twice-daily watering. Standing pots in trays with a little water is a help during dry periods, and the trays will act as reservoirs in showery weather, but they must be emptied during longer periods of rain, or plants may become waterlogged.

Airborne pests such as aphids and blackflies can present a real problem in the still atmosphere of an enclosed garden, as once they have landed they will not move. They do the greatest damage to the young shoots of plants that are under stress (for example, through lack of water); so the most useful precaution you can take is to make sure plants are healthy and growing well. If you do discover a colony smothering a plant, wipe them off and crush every one of them – I do it with my bare fingers, but use a cloth or gloves if you find that too disgusting. If the attack is widespread I spray the insects with liquid detergent (which has the added bonus of reviving the plants), but inevitably a few escape, and I always have to do some follow-up squashing. I try never to resort to chemicals in a restricted space; even apart from the environmental dangers, it would mean yet more bottles to store.

In many towns and cities cats are among the worst pests. They dig holes where you have just seeded your favourite summer annuals, and they always choose a newly planted climber to spray on, or lie down in the middle of a treasured shrub. There are few reliable remedies. Cat pepper helps a bit, but soon leaches away. In *Down the Garden Path* Beverley Nichols recounts his success with treacle put in pools along the top of the garden wall – but I have never tried this technique, so cannot vouch for its efficacy! If you are unfortunate enough to live in an area where the cat population is high, probably the best solution is to have your own cat, which should at least keep most others away.

To look after your garden properly you will need a few good tools – if only a broom, watering can, secateurs, a trowel or small spade and a fork. In all but the tiniest of gardens, space should be made for a shed to accommodate them; otherwise they will always be in the way and take up precious space in the house. Include the shed in the overall design of the garden: try to hide it and you condemn it to becoming the shabby hut so often seen. The cheap structures available at most garden centres can be painted attractively – in a buff tone sponged over with a creamy colour, for example. If you fix some trellis, painted in the same way, to support a climbing rose, your storage space can become a garden feature.

GARDEN STYLE

In gardening, style is a matter of creating a sense of order and harmony between many different components. Ultimately the style of a garden is a reflection of its designer's taste and personality. But the garden's style must also be guided by its setting – the house it belongs to, and, in the case of an urban garden, the surrounding town or city.

How do you choose an appropriate style for your garden? The architectural style of the house is often a useful guide. Generally speaking, it is only for reasons of historical curiosity that we would wish to produce a perfect replica of, say, an eighteenth-century formal garden, keeping rigidly to planting plans of the period; for our own gardens most of us prefer something more eclectic. However, a garden in a style that derives broadly from a particular period is often effective, and the process of creating such a garden is fascinating. A single

period feature – perhaps a tiny knot garden, an arbour, or a piece of sculpture – can set the tone. Taking the date of the house as a starting point, you might embark on a little research. Plans of historical gardens can be found in specialist libraries, and paintings, prints and antiquarian books are good sources of period details. Remembering that just as the house will have been altered to suit different generations so will the garden, you can adapt the plan to your own circumstances.

Sometimes the original style of the architecture is so lost in alterations that its character is no longer identifiable, or the site has changed greatly in size and surroundings, or the garden style of the appropriate period is incompatible with your needs. You may decide to create a garden in the idiom of quite a different period, or to pursue the garden style of another country, or to follow a theme of colour or mood. The choice is yours. But it is worth trying to identify a style or theme that will help you to make the garden into a cohesive whole.

Regrettably, the architecture of a town house is sometimes not at all attractive, and provides quite an unsuitable backdrop to the garden. It may be possible to make improvements to the house itself, but even quite small alterations tend to be costly, and camouflage is often the only feasible recourse. On the other hand, a town house can be lovely, and then every opportunity must be taken to emphasize and highlight its beauty. Many houses are a mixture, with the front well appointed for all the world to see, while the back has been left unadorned to save on building costs.

Left A small statue of a boy on a fluted plinth inspires a contemplative mood in an intimate corner of this garden. Camellias provide an evergreen backdrop, while hardy ferns and tender *Pilea cadierei* complete the leafy setting.

Right An entrance arch of clipped *Thuja plicata* and symmetrically shaped beds edged with low hedges of box (*Buxus sempervirens* 'Suffruticosa') set

the formal tone of this garden. In the centre of each bed is a clipped box ball, surrounded by lavender and silvery-leaved plants including *Stachys lanata* and artemisia. The style echoes that of a sixteenth-century knot garden, and although the central balustered bird bath is of a much later date, it looks entirely appropriate.

Effective camouflage is not easy to achieve. The aim is not to smother an object with a mantle of greenery, but rather to make it merge into the background, with the plants and ornaments standing out against it and catching the eye. It pays to start with a good clean slate. Dirty walls should be cleaned, and an unattractively plain wall surface is often greatly improved by a coat of paint. Choose your colour carefully. The freshness of white may seem appealing, but white is really only suitable for hot, dry countries where the light intensity is high and sharp contrasts are necessary; besides, in most towns and cities, white soon loses its pristine crispness. In countries where the weather is often damp and overcast, pale pink, buff-orange or cream will look softer and warmer, and be more durable. Alternatively, a grey, beige-stone or, more subtly, one colour sponged on to another, say muddy green on beige or cream on pink, can look surprisingly good.

A trellis attached to the wall will have the effect of making the wall itself fade further into the background. It is usually best for the trellis to be in the same colour as the wall: contrasting colours tend to attract attention, thus defeating the object of the exercise. For a grand scheme it may be worth considering *trompe-l'œil* trelliswork, but beware: if it is not to be disturbing to the eye, *trompe-l'œil* needs to be very well done. Trellis, of course, will serve as a support to plants you may choose to grow up the wall, and can also be used for screening elsewhere in the garden, serving as a linking element in the garden design.

Using trellis to raise the height of walls often provides an effective solution to the problem of camouflaging ugly structures outside the garden. But one medium-sized upright tree, or a summerhouse in the right position, may be enough to divert the eye. Great barriers of vegetation and masonry should be avoided in small spaces.

Left A subtle colour scheme restricted to warm blues, pinks and mauves unifies this shady courtyard garden (featured on pages 98–9). The walls have been painted, using a sponging technique, to look weathered, and to harmonize with the basket-weave brick paving. The pendulous mauve racemes of the ancient wisteria, seen here in full flower, seem to have been the inspiration and the starting point for the garden, and in this subdued setting its tortuous stems take on a sculptural role.

Right Trellis rising above the top of a garden wall not only supports climbing plants, it also screens views beyond. In this city garden (featured on pages 120–21) tall shrubs and trees disguise the boundaries and concentrate interest on the wealth of planting at ground level.

Enhancing a beautiful building requires equal care. Discretion is the key to success here, and I would always go for the more restrained climbers and flowering wall shrubs, such as large-flowered clematis, *Camellia* 'St Ewe' and *Chaenomeles japonica*. When you choose your plants you should give some thought to the design and general architectural lines of the house and to the habit of the plant. Positively upright shrubs such as *Magnolia grandiflora* should only be planted against a tall, uninterrupted piece of wall where they will not need to be diverted around windows; on the other hand, horizontal shrubs, such as *Cotoneaster horizontalis*, can serve to emphasize the lines of the windows. It is wise to avoid using too many different types of plants; a muddle would just detract from the appearance of the house.

Entrances to the house should be carefully framed. Urns, obelisks or topiary specimens look well in formal gardens, and in more informal situations scented plants are delightful: you might try the early-flowering *Daphne mezereum*, the climbing *Trachelospermum asiaticum*, or, if you want an evergreen, *Osmanthus delavayi* or *Choisya ternata*.

Growing scented plants near the door is one of the ways of bringing the garden right into the house. The scent heralds more to come, and beckons you on. Each time of the year has a perfume of its own. Winter smells are sharp and sweet, all the more precious for being so few. The scents of *Lonicera fragrantissima*, *Hamamelis mollis* and *Chimonanthus praecox* are among my favourites. Most of the winter-flowering shrubs do not have a lot to commend them during the rest of the year, so, to make the most of the space they occupy, try growing over them some showy climbers, such as clematis. In a town garden there are rarely enough winter flowers to pick and bring into the house, but in pots *Iris reticulata* followed by the true jonquil, *Narcissus jonquilla*, can be appreciated at close quarters.

In spring the flowers are larger and more showy. One shrub of *Viburnum carlesii* will fill a small garden with a rich perfume. The clusters of white blossoms open at tulip time (they are followed in the autumn, if the summer is long and hot, by bunches of black fruit). Later in spring will come *Clematis montana*, lilac and lily of the valley, and then, to herald the summer, the heavy fragrance of wisteria.

Right An abundance of fuchsias, growing in pots and attached to wall-mounted trellis, makes this enclosed entrance seem light and airy. In spring the pots are filled with bulbs and pansies, while the foliage of the ivy, ferns and other plants grown in the large terracotta containers gives continuity to the design and provides all-year-round interest.

Far left An entrance framed by arches gives an impression of depth. The arch around the front door of this house is echoed at the entrance to the garden, where the vigorous golden hop *Humulus lupulus* 'Aureus' scrambles over another arch. A more formal pergola next to the house supports a number of other rambling plants, including clematis and *Akebia quinata*. The axis to the door is defined by a pair of clipped yew pillars, two standard box balls in pots, and a *Choisya ternata*, placed near the house for protection from frost.

Left In this formal approach, a paved and cobbled pathway is lined with a box hedge. Simple terracotta pots on stone plinths, placed on either side of the front step, complete the careful framing of the door and enhance its classic formality. A vigorous *Hydrangea petiolaris* softens the straight lines.

The summer garden is filled with scents that mingle to give rich sensations. Roses, of course, are among the main ingredients. Some of the best of the climbing cultivars that are appropriate in a small garden are 'New Dawn', 'Climbing Ena Harkness', 'Zéphirine Drouhin' and 'Veilchenblau'. Sweet honeysuckle, particularly *Lonicera japonica* (the type species, not the golden-netted form), will intertwine with roses, and pungent rosemary will enjoy the warm conditions at the base of a sunny wall. Other scented herbs include thymes, mints, the unmistakable curry plant (*Helichrysum italicum*) and lemon balm (*Melissa officinalis*). Among other lemon-scented plants my favourites are pelargoniums, particularly the cultivar 'Mabel Grey', and lemon verbena (*Aloysia citriodora*). Both are tender, but worth growing in pots so that they can be brought into the house or conservatory in winter; even when picked the leaves retain their aroma for a long time. Summer evenings can be delightfully fragrant, with *Jasminum polyanthum*, evening primrose, night-scented stock, tobacco plants and double rocket all coming into their own at dusk.

The scents of autumn are more elusive. There will still be the evergreen herbs to brush against, and a few lingering summer blooms. The late-flowering *Clerodendrum trichotomum*, with fragrant blossom followed by glowing blue berries, is a good autumn shrub for the town garden.

The style and atmosphere of your garden will be influenced greatly by the colours you choose. I like the discipline colours impose on the design. Generally I prefer to combine different colours, rather than restricting myself to tones of one. I do try never to mix more than three colours together, and I usually follow the broad guidelines of some of the classic combinations, including blue and pale yellow, pink and pale blue with silver foliage, purple and lemon yellow, warm red and deeper yellow. But it is fun to experiment with contrasting and complementary colours, and I often find that I come across the best combinations by accident. I particularly enjoy the way a painting, an illustration in a book, a new plant or a planting seen in someone else's garden will open one's eyes to the possibility of a fresh and intriguing colour association.

I would always advise you to look for the unusual and aim to make a bold statement, rather than err on the safe side with plain and diffuse colours and common plant associations. Provided that you have established a strong framework in hues of green, you can be as adventurous as you like. If you have doubts about an effect, you can try out your ideas using bulbs and annuals before introducing more permanent plantings.

Above A strong framework of vigorous ivy makes a permanent backdrop to the changing colour schemes in this garden. Here white azaleas match the garden furniture and small patches of pink soften the dark green background, but for the moment the dominant presence, in colour and scent, is a cascade of fragrant mauve wisteria.

Right In this deliciously scented garden, the perfumes of roses, honeysuckle, philadelphus, lavender and *Lilium regale* are all intermingled. The fragrant theme begins in spring with the *Clematis armandii* that scrambles over the pergola. The cupola, which came from the top of an old building, provides an unusual and strong focal point.

As you plan your garden for colour and scent, consider, too, variations in shape and texture. Think for a moment of leaves alone: there are soft hairy leaves, hard leathery ones, they come small and spiny, large and round, sharply sword-shaped, gracefully heart-shaped. Add to these the shapes and textures of flowers and you will have some idea of the variety of possible combinations offered by the gardener's palette.

Whenever you choose a plant, try to visualize its effect on the garden throughout the year. When you select a shrub, for instance, think not only of its appearance when it is in flower, but also of the autumn hues of turning leaves and ripening berries, and the quality of the bark in winter. Choose plants that will complement and succeed each other, to ensure that there is always life and interest in form and colour throughout the seasons.

Finally, do spend time in your garden looking after it. More than anything else, this will help you to achieve your aim of conveying a sense of harmony. As you water, weed, prune and keep a vigilant eye open for pests and diseases, you will not only keep the garden in order, you will also get to know the space, and develop a feeling for its character and requirements.

Above left This simple composition in the corner of a paved garden is rich in shapes and textures. A russet-coloured Japanese maple reaches across a tree peony to a hydrangea, while a symphoricarpos arches over the needle-like foliage of evergreen candytuft. A glossy birch trunk provides a strong vertical accent.

Above At the front of a sunny spring border, the variegated leaves of Our Lady's thistle (*Silybum marianum*) catch the light. Behind, the clear outlines of tulips – lily-flowered 'White Triumphator' and the pink double 'Angélique' – are emphasized by the background of *Rhamnus alaternus* 'Argenteovariegata'.

An abundance of ground cover and climbing plants brings a country air to this town garden (featured on pages 120–21). Geraniums and silver-leaved stachys grow in drifts, spilling over the paved path, and a mass of *Campanula poscharskyana* obscures the base of the trellis. While the blue flowers of the iris harmonize with the colours of these plants, its sharply pointed foliage contrasts with their softness. Climbing roses in warm tones of red, pink and apricot disguise the garden's boundaries, and, beyond the trellis, the grey foliage and yellow flowers of a santolina catch the sunlight.

CREATING THE FRAMEWORK

Aim for simplicity in the basic structure of your garden. A framework with clear, bold lines allows for freedom in the detail. The success of the design will depend on whether the proportions are appropriate to the area available, with the provisos that, however small, the garden must be to the human scale, and should include a variety of elements and have a sense of space. For example, a substantial pergola across the garden will divide a formal paved area from an informal one, while framing vistas from one to the other.

A SENSE OF SPACE

Even in the smallest of gardens, it is possible to create a feeling of space. One way is to use elements that decrease in size towards the back of the garden; because these features are smaller than those nearer the house they seem further away than they actually are, and this gives an illusion of depth. Narrower openings, shrubs that are gradually reduced in height and width, even smaller grades of gravel all contribute to this effect. Plants can be used in the same way: for example, the tiny leaves of rue (*Ruta graveolens*), will appear further away for being planted at the end of a path edging of lady's mantle (*Alchemilla mollis*), with its large, round leaves. Colour plays a part too. The bluer the shade, the more it appears to recede into the background – so choose the best form of rue, *R. graveolens* 'Jackman's Blue', and the end of your garden will seem even more remote. At the other end of the spectrum, red appears to advance and shorten distance. An area of large red leaves at the bottom of a long, thin garden will do a lot, visually, to improve the proportions.

Mirrors have manifold uses in a small garden. Positioned in a wall, like a window or a door, a mirror not only provides light, it also gives an impression of increased space and depth. A sheet of aluminium foil behind an old pane of glass, made watertight at the edges, is all that is needed: brand new plate mirror can appear hard and discordant when you are trying to create a peaceful atmosphere. A grand effect can be achieved by positioning a pair of statues, pots or topiary specimens so that they are reflected in the glass. You can even double the perspective by placing a second mirror on an opposite wall.

Above A brick archway appears to frame an enticing glimpse of a vista that lies beyond. In fact, the impression that the generous planting extends into the distance is a charming illusion. The arch is lined with a mirror, its edges blurred by clematis and Virginia creeper (*Parthenocissus quinquefolia*), and the view is a reflection of the garden.

Right In a shady corner of a paved garden, a dilapidated mirror, set in a bricked-up opening and flanked by two classical columns, reflects, and helps create, a picture of melancholy, romantic charm. The mirror brings depth, mystery and a soft light, and its stained surface is delightfully in keeping with the scene.

Surprisingly enough, dividing the garden up will also give a sense of space, even as it creates a feeling of intimacy. The best town gardens that I have visited are broken up into smaller units, each with its own theme. There may, for example, be a terrace, a pergola for climbers, a herb garden, and a little shrubbery. The feeling of space comes from the way not all of the garden is seen at once: although the area you stand in may be smaller, you know there is more beyond. A suggestion of what is to come will entice you to explore further. Windows and gateways in partitions invite you to discover hidden treasures, steps usher you on to a different level from which you will see the garden in a excitingly new way.

The feeling of moving into a different area is dramatically increased by a change of level – to the extent that, on a flat site, it may be worth lowering one area and raising another. On a sloping site, terracing makes a much more positive statement than just allowing the ground to run away, seemingly out of control. Each terrace can have a theme or pattern within the overall style of the garden. For example, in an Italianate garden you could have a water garden on one level with a parterre on the next and terracotta pots and statues on a third. In a wild garden there could be a pond garden on one level, a butterfly garden on the second and a meadow garden on the third.

Retaining walls to accommodate changes of level must be well constructed, capable of supporting the load of earth behind, and with adequate drainage. The material chosen, whether brick, wood, stone or concrete, should be in sympathy with the fabric of the house, and with other garden features. Holes for rock or wall plants, each with its little pocket of earth, can be incorporated in the construction, and a narrow bed along the top of the wall will offer another opportunity for growing plants that thrive in well-drained conditions.

This steeply sloping garden in the town of Tarascon, in southern France, has been terraced to create several clearly defined levels. Lining the boundary walls and the steps are raised beds brimming with jasmine, honeysuckles (*Lonicera japonica* 'Halliana' and *L.* × *heckrottii* 'Gold Flame') and roses including 'Wedding Day'. The raised pool on the top terrace is matched by another below, a device that helps to unify the design.

Terracing the site produces additional planting space, which can be a great advantage in a small garden. The brick retaining walls here are substantial and neatly constructed. The reclaimed materials give an air of maturity, and the stone capping and the antique urn impart a strong outline, against which the planting stands out well. The various levels can accommodate plants with different needs: the pool at the bottom is surrounded by moisture-loving primulas and irises, while in the top bed *Juniperus horizontalis*, a variegated New Zealand flax (*Phormium tenax* 'Variegatum') and a pale yellow shrub rose enjoy the driest position.

Left The old brick wall that marks the boundary of this small, narrow garden (featured on pages 90–93) is smothered by a collection of climbers, small shrubs and herbaceous plants. In concealing the wall, this generous abundance conveys the impression that the planting and the garden go far beyond their actual limits. The deep blue clematis 'Lord Nevill' and the rose 'New Dawn', mingling together, link the mahogany-red palmate foliage of *Heuchera* 'Palace Purple', the tall flower spikes of *Nepeta govaniana* and the deeply veined leaves of *Hosta sieboldiana*. Beyond are the camellia 'Leonard Messel', which flowers in late winter, and the finger-like leaves of *Rhododendron yakushimanum*.

Right The boundary of this New York penthouse garden is defined by substantial trellis panels punctuated by large wooden planters, all painted a gleaming white.

Far right Wooden panels that were specially designed to fit the space mark the boundaries of this garden. The raised patterns have been varied to define different areas, while the continuous frieze unifies the construction. Hydrangeas in large terracotta pots soften an otherwise stark corner.

BOUNDARIES

As both frame and background to a garden, boundaries must be a major consideration. The boundaries of a small town garden need especially careful treatment. It takes planning to achieve a sense of privacy without having to plant a forest that takes up the whole space, and to hide outside intrusions without losing attractive features, such as neighbouring trees and shrubs, that could be included in your scheme.

The boundaries may be blurred with plants, marked clearly with walls or fencing, or simply indicated with markers. Generally, in a town garden, a wall or fence makes a more suitable boundary than a hedge, which lacks the architectural strength appropriate to an urban setting, and takes up a lot of space in what is probably a small area. However, if a hedge is your preferred alternative, I would advise you to choose plants such as yew or holly, that can be clipped into solid, formal shapes. When planting your hedge, remember to prepare the ground thoroughly and incorporate plenty of slow-release fertilizer around the roots.

In a walled garden, the walls will be the background against which the garden stands. If you are building a new wall, choose materials that are sympathetic to the materials of the house, and the town or city, and that have character. In a town where the vernacular material for houses is the local stone, this will usually be the best choice. For a brick wall, it is worth seeking out old handmade bricks: they have a patina of their own, and, moreover, they can be bought, secondhand, more cheaply than machine-made modern ones.

It is more likely, however, that you will have inherited your wall with the garden. If you have a wall of old stone or mellowed brick you are fortunate. It is a waste to smother a beautiful surface with vigorous climbers; rather, use the opportunity to grow more restrained plants that will be set off by a fine backcloth. And take full advantage of the microclimate offered by the wall. Benefiting as you do from the warming influence of being in a town, if you also have a wall that receives a generous amount of light you may well find you can succeed with plants that are considered tender for the area. Many plants are quite hardy once they are established and by providing additional

protection in winter while they are young, you can pull them through the vulnerable early years. Straw, peat or forest bark piled over the base of the plant gives protection to the roots and young shoots, which may grow up the following season if others die back. A sheet of glass, as well as keeping the worst of the cold out, prevents excessive rain from soaking the roots, so they are less likely to freeze or rot off in the dormant season. Some of the plants which, given this protection, may thrive are *Embothrium coccineum*, *Clematis armandii*, *Campsis radicans*, *Magnolia grandiflora* and, in warmer climates, *Bougainvillea*.

Among other plants that will grace an attractive wall are large-flowered clematis, japonica (*Chaenomeles speciosa*), honeysuckles (winter, spring and summer-flowering species), the everlasting pea (*Lathyrus latifolius*), the bulbous glory lily (*Gloriosa superba*), which makes a magnificent show throughout the summer, and, of course, roses. A pale pink or orange-buff rose, for example 'Kathleen Harrop' or 'Gloire de Dijon', looks charming on a red brick wall, while the deep red 'Copenhagen' or pink 'Madame Grégoire Staechelin' complements a

Below left In this garden specially structured trellis panels have been attached to a flat wall to create the illusion that the wall is angled: the garden appears larger and assumes a more interesting shape. Chain link fencing on the top of the wall gives additional screening.

Below right In a small Washington garden (featured on pages 116–19), a fake stone wall and an arch complete with classical pillars and pediment frame an ancient statue that gazes into the depths of a pool. In reality, both wall and arch are made of wood: the wall has been painted and scored to resemble granite blocks, the arch painted to look like limestone. The wall is just 1.5m/5ft high and the pediment of the arch only rises to 2.5m/8ft. No attempt is made to hide the large barn behind: instead a flowering dogwood (*Cornus florida*) has been planted to match one in a neighbouring garden, and to distract the eye from the barn. On either side of the statue handsome pots hold standard wisterias underplanted with ivy.

It is hard to believe that this dramatic scene has been created almost entirely on a flat wall. Only the horizontal balustrade and the statue are real; the rest of the composition was painted by the artist Roy Alderson. Different techniques were used to achieve the required effect. The pinkish stonework at the top was painted on melamine, while the steps, their balustrading and the urns are in yellow ochre acrylic paint on plaster. The edges of the painting are blurred by climbers including *Jasminum officinale*, *Parthenocissus henryana*, *Hedera helix* and *Humulus lupulus* 'Aureus', all vigorous plants that need frequent pruning to prevent them from engulfing the painting.

grey stone wall. There are also annual climbers, such as the cup and saucer plant (*Cobaea scandens*), that can be grown from seed. In a colder climate or a shaded area of the garden, the robust and tolerant *Hydrangea petiolaris* is a good choice; or, for a really stunning effect, you could try the wall shrub *Pyracantha coccinea*, with the large-leaved ivy *Hedera colchica* 'Dentata Variegata' growing through it.

Fruit trees can be trained against the wall in an espalier, to make the most of sunshine and for decorative effect. Figs, peaches and apricots all have attractive foliage, and in a warm climate you may also get a good crop of fruit. In colder conditions, you might prefer apples or plums. Many fruit trees can be grown on dwarfing rootstocks to reduce their vigour and size. Remember that whatever the plants, if the material of the walls is part of the design of the garden, the vegetation must not be allowed to hide it: regular use of the secateurs is essential.

The reality is that the majority of town garden walls are not beautiful, and will benefit from treatment or camouflage. Dirty walls can be cleaned, plain walls painted; a trellis attached to the wall relieves monotony, and will support climbers.

Or, for really thoroughgoing disguise, you might consider a mural. A well-executed mural adds depth to your garden – and you can choose just the garden extension you want: a woodland glade, formal topiary, monumental architecture or colourful bedding. Remember though, that painted gardens do not evolve, over the years or over the seasons. A herbaceous border might be cheerful to look at in winter, but it would seem incongruous, and could easily become irritating. It is usually better to stick to evergreens, or to architectural details. Treat your mural with conviction: steps leading to a painted urn in a niche will strengthen its impact; and if the steps are used to display pots, the edges between real and unreal will be further blurred. A dummy door in a wall can totally divert attention from the wall itself, particularly if it is flanked by columns that are set slightly forward. The illusion is all the more convincing if the door is glazed with panes of mirror.

Climbers such as roses and clematis that adorn a lovely wall will also embellish an ugly one. If you want something more fast-growing, and concealing, try evergreens such as ivies, pyracantha or *Euonymus fortunei radicans*, or, for autumn colour, *Celastrus orbiculatus* or the glory vine (*Vitis coignetiae*). Again, remember that plants chosen for their vigour and speed of growth need regular attention and pruning; there is a fine line between a luxuriant garden and a garden that looks neglected and overgrown.

Fences provide a cheaper alternative to walls, and are more usual in modern town gardens. A simple picket or palisade is attractive, and provides a good background for light climbers such as sweet peas, clematis, honeysuckle, roses and the climbing nasturtiums *Tropaeolum peregrinum* and *T. speciosum*. On the other hand, some fences, particularly those of the solid type with overlapping boards, are hideous, and the only recourse is to hide them behind a bold planting of shrubs. Viburnums such as *Viburnum opulus* and *V. × burkwoodii* and cornus such as *Cornus mas* and *C. alba* 'Elegantissima' have the required bulk. Smaller rhododendron hybrids, such as *Rh.* P.J.M., 'Dora Amateis' or 'Blue Peter', will provide flowers in spring and evergreen foliage throughout the year; if you add a philadelphus and *Abelia × grandiflora* you can have flowers through the summer and into the autumn; and *Mahonia japonica* will contribute clusters of scented yellow flowers in winter.

FOCAL POINTS

Include in your design a focal point that draws and holds the attention, and acts as a climax for the whole garden. This may be a piece of sculpture or an ornament, a plant or a group including plants, a water feature, or a garden structure such as an arbour or summerhouse. The focal point may change according to the hour of the day and the season, as the sunlight is more or less intense in different parts of the garden. Each smaller, self-contained area should also have its focus.

An interesting sculpture is a good focal point for a walled town garden. Protected from the distractions of incompatible surroundings, it will set the mood and underline the chosen theme. Decide, before you choose your sculpture, what general mood you want to create. For example, the classical lines characteristic of the eighteenth century are appropriate in a cool, restrained, composed atmosphere, while the heavier, more insistent lines of the late nineteenth century will contribute to a more flamboyant effect.

Above A white-painted palisade fence is elegantly clothed by the pale pink climbing rose 'New Dawn', and complemented by the tall, straight stems of a bamboo and the delicate foliage of a fern.

Right Gail Jenkins, who owns this Melbourne garden, created this vista to be viewed from her kitchen window. The eye is led straight through the grape vine archway, up the grass path edged with *Lavandula stoechas*, to the small stone statue that stands amidst a sea of *Erigeron karvinskianus*. This garden is full of roses. Above the statue is the standard rose 'Sea Foam', while 'Madame Isaac Pereire', 'Boule de Neige', 'Climbing Iceberg', 'Zéphirine Drouhin' and 'Variegata di Bologna' climb over the posts and the rope swags, and 'Albertine' flowers exuberantly at the garden's boundary.

The range of statues and ornaments available extends from fine antiques and the work of established contemporary artists – eminently desirable, but too expensive for most of us – to moulded plastic urns. The cast stone, imitation bronze and lead reproductions that fall into the intermediate category are often roughly made, and not always modelled on the best examples; however, some are pleasing and of good quality. If you would prefer an original work, you could try contacting a local art college. You may well find a student whose style you like, and who is happy to make you a sculpture at a price you can afford.

Only a plant of permanent architectural beauty – a topiary yew or box specimen, perhaps, or *Phormium tenax* with its huge, sword-like leaves – will hold its own throughout the year as the focus of a garden. A plant such as *Magnolia stellata*, *Acer palmatum* or *Cornus alba* 'Sibirica' can be a focal point during its moment of glory; after that, the focus must move elsewhere. A seasonal plant may be most effective when used to support a focal point. I was once struck by the association of a simple terracotta pot and a wisteria in full flower on a nearby pergola: while for most of the year the pot was just one among many garden ornaments, during its flowering the wisteria led the eye directly to the pot, making it the focal point of the garden.

WATER FEATURES

The presence of water in a garden contributes to an atmosphere of peace and tranquillity, and a water feature – a fountain, water cascading or trickling from a mask mounted on a wall, a simple pool – makes a fascinating focal point. The natural movement of the water coupled with the play of light creates patterns that are constantly changing; and in a town or city garden, the sound of fountains and rills even goes some way towards masking traffic noise. A pool will reflect the sky and bring light into a gloomy courtyard, or can be used specifically to reflect a statue, an urn or another architectural feature. As a further attraction, the water will be a draw to wildlife, from insects and frogs to birds, and, herons and cats permitting, you can keep fish.

The site and style of your water piece will be influenced by various factors. First, there is the practical matter of how and where you can get water into the garden. Then, do you want the water to be still or running? If you have a choice, do you want it to be in a sunny or a shady area? The design must be in keeping with the amount of available light: a grotto with water trickling slowly down rocks would look completely wrong in bright sun,

Right Water spouting from a lion's head mounted on the wall makes an attractive focal point in this shady corner. The mask is surrounded by the glossy foliage of *Hydrangea petiolaris* with, beneath, pale pink and magenta impatiens, deeply veined hostas, and the silver-variegated leaves of *Lamiastrum galeobdolon* 'Variegatum'.

Far left A classical bust on a stone column makes a strong focal point, marking the termination of an axis flanked by two rows of box pyramids. In summer the line of box is emphasized by a planting of blue and white petunias that add a touch of restrained colour to the composition.

Left A reproduction of a pensive figure in a wide-brimmed feathered hat, believed to be an early eighteenth-century French sculpture, sets the restful tone of this garden. Raised on a plinth, it stands out as a focal point above a display of white hydrangeas.

where a flat pool with a fountain gaily playing would be delightfully appropriate. Decide how formal or informal you want your water feature to be. Remember that you cannot venture too far into the realm of informality on a terrace where the features are essentially architectural and therefore rigid and formal. But you can have an irregularly shaped pool with carefully chosen plants – or, alternatively, you can have a strictly regular geometric pond, with a central fountain and no plants at all. On a tiny scale, you can simply remove a single slab from an area of paving and make a little pool in the space.

The courtyards of the Alhambra, in Spain, are a wonderfully rich source of ideas for water features. The three famous courtyards are an inspiration – their water effects glories to feast our eyes on and dream about, though hardly to reproduce. In the Court of the Mosque a circular fluted basin set low within an octagonal overflow channel is sunk in the white marble floor. The Court of the Pool has a central long, rectangular pool that has recently been planted on either side with beds of clipped myrtle; at either end is a low circular pool with a central bubbly fountain. The richly decorated Court of the Lions, surrounded by triple-arched colonnades, has a twelve-sided marble fountain basin supported by twelve carved lions from whose mouths pour jets of water.

Also interesting, and surprisingly easy to imitate in a small town courtyard or on a terrace, are the many smaller enclosures and incidental fountains and pools. The shapes and combinations seem endlessly varied: a flat, dark, rectangular pool with semicircles cut out of the sides is set in paving and surrounded by a low hedge; a raised stone circular pool has a central baluster supporting a shallow basin with a fountain in the middle; a lotus-shaped basin with a bubbling fountain is supported by a column set in a low octagonal overflow pool and surrounded by myrtle balls planted in hand-thrown, wobbly terracotta pots. Wall fountains dribble into a raised rectangular stone tank that is permanently overflowing and has developed a patina of dark green moss.

Whatever their shape or type, pools and tanks should always be filled to capacity: they look neglected when they are only half full of water. In a purely ornamental pool, the water need not be deep – making the inside of a pool black is enough to create an impression of limitless depth. Fish, however, need at least 20cm/8in. of water.

Left The straight lines of this rectangular pool are softened by the plants that billow over the edges. Roses and hydrangeas provide a flowering backdrop to meconopsis, tradescantia, geraniums and stachys, while by the brick path two clipped box balls add a note of definition.

Right A stream opens out into a wide pool, beside a deck of wide planks that links the house and the water, providing a peaceful place to sit and relax. A narrow stone bridge joins the terrace to the garden, spanning the pool at its widest point. Two tall cypresses flank the house and introduce height to the composition, and margins of grass and white gravel mark the curve of the water.

Water plants can be difficult to manage, so it is generally better to concentrate on just a few. Water lilies (*Nymphaea* species) lend an air of grandeur to a formal pond, while the floating plants golden club (*Orontium aquaticum*) and water soldiers (*Stratiotes aloides*) are better for a natural-looking pool. You will need to include some oxygenating plants, to avoid a build-up of algae. Try water violet (*Hottonia palustris*) or water crowfoot (*Ranunculus aquatilis*). They both need regular thinning in autumn to prevent excessive spread, but they are not nearly so invasive as the Canadian pondweed (*Elodea canadensis*), or common duckweed (*Lemna minor*).

There are also many plants that will thrive in the damp margins of a pond. Some of these are species that are found in boggy conditions in the wild: they include the marsh marigold (*Caltha palustris*), water irises such as *Iris laevigata* and the yellow flag (*I. pseudacorus*), pickerel weed (*Pontederia cordata*), and Japanese butterbur (*Petasites japonicus*). Others are plants that generally like cool shade but, with moisture, will also do well in sun. Among them are brunnera, hostas, astilbes, creeping jenny and trilliums.

GARDEN STRUCTURES

A well-chosen structure makes an effective focal point for a garden; simply as part of the general scene, it can contribute height, style, individuality, aplomb and maturity. Remember that any garden structure, whether it is a pergola, an arbour or summerhouse or a simple archway over a gate, must be well made and substantial enough to stand on its own during the winter months, unadorned by the climbers that may clothe it during the summer.

If you want to bring a country style to your town garden, you could have a simple wooden wicket gate topped with a basic iron arch, framing the view beyond and supporting honeysuckle and clematis which change with the seasons. At the other extreme, an elaborate wrought or cast-iron gate set in a brick or stone wall has a sophisticated air, and would be more appropriate if you have an eighteenth or nineteenth-century town house. The shape of the arch can be rounded or square, gothic or classical, depending on the style and period of the house, but it should be well proportioned.

Right An ornate white ironwork gate leads from a shady fern-filled conservatory, with a rather nineteenth-century atmosphere, to the sunny terrace that lies beyond. The open pattern of the gate's ironwork allows enticing glimpses out on to Sydney harbour.

Left A simple wicket gate, with a country air, divides a private town garden from the communal grounds beyond. The *Thuja plicata* arch leads into a formally laid out garden with box-edged beds (shown on page 33).

Below This substantial summerhouse is constructed of wooden panels that match the panels of the garden's boundaries (shown on page 47). The seat and the Versailles *caisse* are part of the same ensemble and complete the picture. To one side of the summerhouse a large purple *Prunus cerasifera* 'Pissardii' sets off the predominantly blue-grey colour scheme.

Right A light trellis structure in the shape of a classical temple and smothered with climbers frames a seat of curly white ironwork. The 'temple' with its seat makes a white and green focal point for a small patio garden where the planting is mostly white and green.

Far right A simple arbour, clad in white trellis and wreathed with a scented white rambling rose, shelters a white cast-iron and wooden bench. The area surrounding the arbour is defined by stone and brick paving. Primulas (yellow *Primula florindae* and pink *P. vialii*), a tree peony and a purple clematis add touches of colour.

A simple arbour or more substantial summerhouse has a feeling of mystery and romance: even in the most exposed of gardens it can give a sense of solitude. In medieval and Renaissance times arbours were traditionally made of willow or hazel, both woods that bend easily when young, so they can be trained, and they were clothed in green from spring to late summer. These days there is available an array of designs in wood or metal for both arbours and summerhouses. Make sure that the shape is suitable for the style you have chosen for your garden, and that the detailing is of good quality; and position the doorway and any windows or openings to ensure that you get the best views of the garden at the times when you are likely to sit there.

Pergolas offer the possibility of framing views into and out of the garden, and making bold separations between different areas. The plants you choose to grow over a pergola must be vigorous enough to clothe the structure, but not so exuberant that it becomes totally swamped. And remember that the more vigorous the plants the more substantial the pergola will need to be. Choose plants that flower in succession, extending the season of the pergola. For a long-lasting display, you could try a combination that includes some of the early and late-flowering clematis, such as *Clematis macropetala* and *C. tangutica*, spring-flowering *Akebia quinata*, climbing roses such as the yellow 'Lawrence Johnston' and the red 'Danse du Feu', and the crimson glory vine (*Vitis coignetiae*). Wisteria and laburnum need careful training in the early years, to create living tunnels. Their flowering time is brief – but glorious.

SURFACES AND STEPS

The surfaces are a vital part of the framework of the garden, linking and separating different areas both physically and aesthetically. Variation in surface materials and texture is a good way of introducing diversity to the garden and breaking up the space. You may, for example, have a paved area next to the house, and further away a lawn, gravel paths and flower beds.

Many gardeners, particularly in England, seem to feel that a garden without a lawn is hardly worthy of the name. It is true that a good lawn is a pleasing surface that is physically and visually restful. And it is quite possible to have a good lawn in an urban garden, provided that there is enough light and moisture (and space to store a lawn mower). However, the truth is that town and city gardens do tend to be dry and shaded, and if a lawn is attempted in these conditions the results are likely to be highly unsatisfactory. It is often best to opt, instead, for an area of shade-tolerant ground-covering plants, such as ivies, pachysandra and epimediums, in association with paving.

There is a wide choice of possible paving materials, but whatever paving you choose, it must be in harmony with the design of the garden as a whole, and be hard-wearing and properly laid. Terracotta, glazed tiles and marble lend themselves best to hot climates, while brick and stone are more appropriate in colder countries. Cobbles, granite setts, cement slabs, gravel, quarry tiles and wooden decking are other possibilities. Each lends a different atmosphere, but they often look well in association. For example, a terrace might have two crossing axial paths paved in stone meeting in the centre, dividing four areas of brick laid in a herringbone pattern. Or, in a less regular space, you could have two or three areas of concrete slabs linked with large-grade gravel.

Introducing creeping rock plants to a pavement adds a touch of informality. The sibling campanulas *Campanula portenschlagiana* and *C. poscharskyana* will make a delightful show of deep blue through much of the summer; but beware, they both seed themselves with abandon. The little stonecrop (*Sedum acre*), sweet alyssum (*Lobularia maritima*), creeping thyme (*Thymus pseudolanuginosus*), camomile (*Chamaemelum nobile*), and the yellow Welsh poppy (*Meconopsis cambrica*) will all grow in cracks. They withstand differing degrees of treading but usually find a niche where they can survive.

Left In a Japanese-style garden screened by a reed fence, wooden decking is combined with gravel and larger, smoother stones to provide pleasantly varied surfacing. Near the wooden path, the delicate tracery of *Acer palmatum* 'Dissectum Atropurpureum' contrasts with, on one side, the sword-like leaves of *Phormium cookianum*, and, on the other, heart-shaped *Hosta sieboldiana*.

Right Gravel paths and dry-stone walling contrast with lush foliage planting, in a garden designed by Ryan Gainey in Atlanta, Georgia. In the central bed lily turf borders azaleas that make a cloud of greenery around a statue of Pegasus.

Clearly defined edges underline and give crispness to the pattern of garden surfaces. A continuous row of low-growing compact plants makes an attractive edging: box (*Buxus sempervirens* 'Suffruticosa') is a traditional edging for a parterre and looks good around borders; border pinks or spiky cushions of *Festuca glauca* are effective in a sunny position; clipped ivy or large-leaved bergenia would be attractive in the shade. Any of these edges can be varied by the introduction at intervals of taller specimen plants, such as topiary subjects or standard flowering shrubs.

There are also many types of hard edging available; choose from them according to the style of your garden. Simple boards on either side of a gravel path keep gravel (or most of it) from running on to paving or flower beds. In the garden of a brick house, hard-baked bricks placed on their sides make an effective edging for paths, borders or a lawn; in a Victorian-style garden the traditional clay rope edge would be appropriate;

split logs help create a rustic effect. Plants such as *Alchemilla mollis*, spilling over on to a path, will soften hard edges.

Steps should always make a bold statement in the garden and be an integral part of the design. They must be comfortable to use: a useful formula stipulates that the breadth of the tread plus twice their depth should equal 66cm/26in.; a depth of 10–18cm/4–7in. is easiest to climb. Within these limits they can be narrow and steep, to be swiftly climbed; or wide and shallow, even, possibly, the width of a small garden, to entice you to linger. They can be used to sit on, or stand pots on; they can be edged with plants or emphasized by a bold balustrade. A flight of steps can form the corner of a small platform; or its base can fan out into a semicircle, concave or convex. Steps from the house to the garden need especially careful planning, to ensure that they make an appropriate link between the two. And they should be as wide as possible, to encourage you to step down or up, and lead you on to discover the delights of the garden.

Steps are used as a feature in this garden, acting as a setting for a collection of plants. In the urn are deep red pelargoniums. The other side of the steps is marked by a standard bay tree (*Laurus nobilis*), with hostas and ferns at its base. On the walls are a rose, a clematis, the variegated ivy *Hedera colchica* 'Dentata Variegata' and a trained × *Fatshedera lizei*. At the top of the steps a shallow sink is filled with saxifrages and sedums.

THE GARDENS

As every gardener knows, other people's gardens are a
wonderful source of inspiration and ideas. In the
following pages town and city gardens from all over the
world are described and illustrated. They are
extremely varied: some are gardens rich in plants,
while others rely primarily on architectural elements;
there are gardens of austere formality and oases of
romantic abundance. Many have been made on tiny
sites and in awkward spaces. Each reflects the
individuality of its owner.

A WELL-FURNISHED GARDEN

When the Jalvings moved into their London house they found a garden that was well established but had for some years received only minimal maintenance, and needed to be replenished. They have breathed new life into it, arranging the basic L-shaped plot to create an impression of separate garden areas, and augmenting the planting with a wealth of new climbers, shrubs and perennials to give year-round interest.

It is a garden for living in as well as for plantsmanship. Nearest the house is a paved area with a table and chairs for eating out and relaxing. The former rectangle of lawn has been contoured into a wide grass path leading from the patio to a circular lawn, which is surrounded by raised beds. From here a circular ironwork pergola acts as a gateway to the pool garden, the design of which is also based on circles. Another set of table and chairs nearby provides an opportunity for enjoying morning sunshine. At night outdoor lighting extends the use of the garden, and illuminates special features.

The garden is fully shaded in winter, and many of the plants have been specially chosen for their winter flowers or foliage. Among the shrubs and trees planted for winter interest are

Prunus × *subhirtella* 'Autumnalis', several pieris, dogwoods, winter jasmine, camellias (*Camellia* 'St Ewe' makes a splendid showing against the studio wall), and viburnums including *Viburnum* × *carlcephalum* and *Viburnum* × *burkwoodii*. In summer flowering shrubs, climbers and a host of perennials fill the garden with colour. At the far, south-facing end the recent collapse and rebuilding of the boundary wall provided the opportunity to enlarge the raised bed at its base, and it has been replanted with an impressive collection of climbing and wall plants in a yellow, white and purple colour scheme.

Left The gentle gurgle of the small fountain in the centre of the pond contributes to the relaxed atmosphere of this London garden. The curve of the brick surround is broken by the heart-shaped dark green leaves of *Zantedeschia aethiopica*, the strap-like leaves of *Iris pseudacorus* 'Variegata' and the feathery ones of *Argyranthemum foeniculaceum*. Water lilies float on the water.

Right An ornate ironwork pergola frames the view across the lawn, where an urn on a pedestal provides a focal point. The grey leaves of helichrysum, tumbling from the urn, contrast with *Hypericum* 'Hidcote' beyond. Smothering the pergola are two roses, the white *Rosa longicuspis* and the palest pink (opening white) 'Aimée Vibert', and three clematis – two dark purple *Clematis* 'Jackmanii Superba' and a pale blue 'William Kennett'. In the shade grow a pink hydrangea and numerous different hostas.

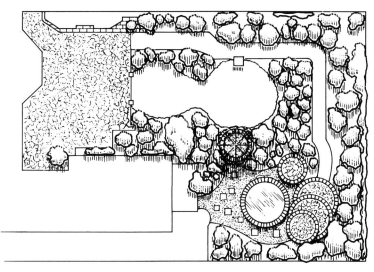

A Secret Garden

Paris is not a city that one normally associates with private gardens, and it always comes as a surprise, as well as a pleasure, to find an oasis of vegetation tucked away behind one of the great facades that line the avenues and side streets. This tiny garden affords an extra shock of delight because the entrance is so unprepossessing: it is only after a walk through a long, dark corridor that the visitor emerges into the light and is greeted with an exuberantly verdant vision of bamboos, a Japanese angelica tree (*Aralia elata*) and Japanese knotweed (*Reynoutria japonica*) against a backdrop of climbers including ivy (*Hedera helix*), Virginia creeper (*Parthenocissus quinquefolia*) and the glory vine (*Vitis coignetiae*).

It is the haven of the landscape gardener Camille Muller, who has transformed a dank and gloomy little courtyard into a luxuriant pleasure garden. He looks out on to it from his apartment at the back of an old building on the edge of Paris's most ancient quarter, the Marais, off the Boulevard St Antoine. The garden is enclosed on three sides, and the low light levels restrict the choice of plants to the most shade-tolerant. But Camille Muller has been so skilful in his selection that all year round there is sufficient variety of foliage to give ample interest. In the summer a few pots of impatiens and pelargoniums add touches of colour at ground level.

But there is another surprise to come: if you look up you will see, balanced on every flat surface of the roof, large boxes full of annuals and tender plants. The climbers planted in the courtyard stretch their stems over the roof and into the sunshine, linking the two levels into one vertical garden. The effect is stunning – well worth the considerable effort that is needed to reach the roof garden through one of the windows of the flat.

Far left In this tiny courtyard, shade-tolerant plants contribute leaves of differing textures, shapes and colours, to provide interest during most of the year. A folding table and chairs, in the sunniest corner, offer an invitation to sit and enjoy this miniature jungle.

Left Above the dormer windows and skylights are large planters brimming over with plants. Impatiens and astilbes flourish in the light shade, climbers from below disguise the planters, and a small bamboo contributes height. Watering takes dedication, as access is through a skylight.

Above A small bust of a lady is the focal point of this little courtyard. Pink pelargoniums growing in pots bring a welcome splash of bright colour among the different tones of green. Climbers including ivy (*Hedera helix*), Virginia creeper (*Parthenocissus quinquefolia*) and Boston ivy (*P. tricuspidata*) clothe the walls and link the courtyard

to the 'garden in the sky' above the dormer windows, where pink petunias and creamy-white tobacco plants in large containers complement the pelargoniums below.

AN INNOVATOR'S GARDEN

The influential and innovatory landscape architect Thomas Church created for his own house in San Francisco a garden that reveals the sure sense of scale and proportion, the wit and the skill that characterize his work. The garden is really two – an imposing entrance garden at the front of the house and a more intimate courtyard at the side. The atmosphere of each is distinct, but they share a sense of privacy and calm.

The entrance garden, hidden from the street by a tall fence and shaded by pollarded *Platanus occidentalis*, has an almost oriental feeling. To one side is a small gravelled patio, its austerity softened by the lushness of the surrounding planting. On the other side a flowing path curves up to an imposing and graceful stairway which divides in two, climbing up on either side of an ivy-covered archway, through which there is access to the courtyard garden. On the steps, tall box bushes pruned into umbrella shapes that rise like fantastic sculptures display Thomas Church's skill in the technique of topiary, as well as his inventiveness in design. Throughout this garden the emphasis is on plants with dramatic shapes or spectacular foliage – pieris, tree ferns, azaleas, aspidistras. Accents of bright colour are provided by plants such as clivias and agapanthus.

Below left Plants used for architectural effect bring a sense of drama to the entrance garden. At the foot of the gracefully curving steps, tall box bushes sculpted into bold umbrella shapes frame a dark, somewhat mysterious-looking ivy-covered archway leading to the courtyard garden.

Below right In the front garden a small stone figure of Summer nestles among clivias planted for their bold, strap-shaped leaves and the vibrant colour of their flowers. Gnarled stems of ivy grown to resemble latticework provide a fantastical backdrop.

Right An overview of the courtyard garden shows how the form of the traditional box parterre has been adapted to suit the small space and emphasize the architectural quality of the design. One end encloses a table and chairs, providing a sense of seclusion for the sitting area, without limiting the overall feeling of space. Nearby, two small stone elephants support pots of seasonal plants.

In the tiny courtyard the feeling is distinctly Mediterranean. Thomas Church was deeply interested in the resemblances he perceived between Mediterranean and Californian gardening conditions – particularly in the way that, in both areas, the climate lends itself to relaxed outdoor living. This garden is a cool, pleasant place to relax and the area occupied by a pretty white-painted table and chairs is quite as integral to the plan as the space for plants.

The design itself is simple. Basically, it is a small rectangular gravel court. The centrepiece, and the element that gives this garden its strong structure, is a box parterre in an abstract design incorporating straight and curved lines. Out of it rise tall rose bushes, and there are more roses in the long, straight bed that runs down one side of the garden. Along the other side, and at the ends, are raised beds with wide wooden edges supporting pots – indeed, there are pots everywhere: in groups on the ground, on ledges, on pedestals and other decorative mounts, and lining steps and borders. In the borders and pots, pale *Primula malacoides* and small-cupped daffodils introduce discreet spring colour; in summer they are succeeded by pink and white pelargoniums. Here, as in the front garden, architectural elements are important and carefully placed: decorative fence posts and balustrades contribute to the framework, and statues rise out of the surrounding foliage.

Right Although the overall design of the courtyard is one of almost classical simplicity, there are many decorative – and often humorous – touches. This corner is adorned by a serene statue and an interesting collection of containers. The whiteness of the intricate latticework surrounding the window brightens the house façade. Next to the window is a visual pun – Thomas Church's 'ironic' column, an Ionic column of iron.

Left In the courtyard, Thomas Church's design brings together plants and artefacts in diverse and interesting shapes. Backed by an imposing balustrade, a statue nestles in the foliage of the rose border. The straight edge of the border directs the eye along the gravel path to a handsome gate, while the sinuous curve of the parterre provides a dramatic contrast.

A GREEN AND WHITE GARDEN

The appeal of this secluded, shady but abundantly verdant garden lies in its masterly groupings of foliage plants punctuated by sculptural focal points. The owner, John Hilton, who designed it himself, had little previous experience of gardening. However, he knew from the beginning that he wanted a garden that looked as good in winter as in summer; that he enjoyed the varying forms and textures of foliage; and that he did not care to introduce any colour other than the many hues of green and white. After a holiday in Japan he decided that vistas, water and acers should play an important part in the total scheme. A background of classical studies influenced his use of columns and sculptures, which act either to draw the eye along a vista or as charming surprises to be discovered and admired at close quarters.

A terrace at the back of the house gives on to a semicircular pool, and then to a lawn with boundaries almost totally

Below left Two weathered urns on classical plinths flank the step from the terrace on to the lawn, where wicker armchairs are placed beneath scented white-flowering jasmine. The pots – one of them containing a young oak tree – can be rearranged according to the season.

Right A handsome domed temple, draped in ivy, provides both a focal point for the garden and a place where family and friends can sit and relax, looking back at the house. To one side, the variegated leaves of *Acer platanoides* 'Drummondii' and

Cornus alba 'Elegantissima' arch over spikes of phormium and yucca – shapes echoed by cordylines in urns by the pillars. To the other side, the massive leaves of a loquat contrast with the rounded forms of clipped *Lonicera nitida* 'Baggesen's Gold' and the soft leaves of *Cupressus sempervirens*.

Left In front of a fluted column half-hidden by ivy, the bust of a bearded man looks out over the terrace and the lawn beyond. A large *Hydrangea petiolaris* covers the north-facing wall of the house and provides a backdrop for the contrasting foliage of plants that include a loquat, a bamboo, *Salix matsudana* 'Tortuosa' and *Acer shirasawanum* 'Aureum'.

Right A white marble bust of a girl on a rough stone column contrasts with a stone pot on an old piece of masonry. The composition is framed by a beech on one side and a camellia on the other, while behind hangs a curtain of the self-clinging vine *Parthenocissus henryana*.

Far right In the most secluded part of the garden a wrought-iron bench is framed by trees and shrubs, and dominated by a tall Corinthian column supporting an eighteenth-century bust of a gentleman. Between the bench and the column stands a Mexican orange (*Choisya ternata*), in a container raised on a chimney pot. The area is screened from view by a large raised bed, constructed of second-hand granite blocks that once paved the streets of London, and filled with shrubs. Here variegated *Cornus alba* 'Elegantissima' stands above the blooms of a white *Hydrangea macrophylla*.

obscured by planting. Two raised beds emphasize the division between the calm, flat lawn and the exuberant plantings, giving each added importance. One bed runs down the length of a boundary wall, the other protrudes boldly to form a peninsula just over half-way across the garden.

The main focal point of the garden is a small temple in the shape of a rotunda, built of Ionic columns and coving rescued from a demolition site, and covered with a fibreglass dome. More fluted stone columns have been used to make a colonnade in the opposite corner of the garden.

The boundaries are brick walls that date back to the mid-nineteenth century, when the house was built. Further height was added to one side by brick piers at 2.5m/8ft intervals, with trellis between them. As well as providing screening from neighbouring houses, this arrangement supplies support for climbers – jasmine and ivies – and a solid background for a collection of white-flowering and variegated shrubs, including a mock orange, a lilac and a variegated fatsia.

John Hilton invested in two mature 7.5m/25ft trees, a western hemlock, (*Tsuga heterophylla*), and a treble-trunked silver birch, (*Betula pendula*), to mitigate the impact of a uniform red brick wall at the end of the garden. Many of the other plants were gifts, or evoke memories of friends and places: a sweet bay, given as a pot plant, that has shot up to 3m/10ft in eight years; a loquat grown from a pip brought back from Spain, a *Trachycarpus* from Japan, an ivy from Venice. The cream-variegated *Acer platanoides* 'Drummondii' and the almost fluorescent *Robinia pseudoacacia* are grown for the drama of their foliage; hogweed, fatsia and a fig for their monumental leaves.

The pond, well stocked with fish and a haven for frogs, provides constant entertainment, as well as the opportunity to grow a range of water plants, again chosen for their interesting foliage or white flowers. The soil dug out to make the pond was used to raise the terrace behind the house. Paved in old York stone, it supports a magnificent collection of plants in terracotta pots that can be moved around according to the season.

A GRACEFUL SOUTHERN GARDEN

The elegant outlines of this garden in Charleston, South Carolina, were drawn up fifty years ago by the landscape architect Loutrell Briggs. They have been filled in, amended, expanded and planted by the owner, Emily Whaley, to make an inspired grouping of separate garden areas that are charming individually, and work as a unified whole.

The 30 × 9m/100 × 30ft plot is a long, narrow rectangle – a shape that is common in city gardens, and can often seem rather corridor-like. Here, the shape has been effectively modified by an underlying design based on circles linked by strong straight lines, with each area symmetrically balanced on either side of the garden's long axis. It is a structure that has stood the test of time, remaining through half a century of changing planting.

An entrance gate from the street opens into an informal area that is entirely Mrs Whaley's own work. It is bounded on two sides by the house, and a pretty stone path, edged with soft clipped mounds of box, winds through it to the rest of the garden. First the path curves round a statue of a girl and a child holding a goose, with a tiny shell pool at their feet, surrounded by *Saxifraga stolonifera* (strawberry begonia) and backed by box (shown on page 127). Next, a backdrop of evergreens with handsome foliage – including *Fatsia japonica*, *Mahonia fortunei*, camellias and azaleas – lends a tropical air to a small pond surrounded by ferns, violets and ajuga. The path ends in a semicircular patio paved with the same stone. It contains decorative seats and pots filled with pelargoniums, impatiens and other bright seasonal flowers.

Left The dramatic shiny green leaves of camellias line the path that winds through the area next to the house, and frame the view beyond. Neat clipped box balls edge the path, and are used to architectural effect throughout the garden, giving structure and distinguishing separate areas. They can be seen marking where the lawn narrows, and outlining the circular area enclosing the pool. Their round shapes are echoed by the mound of ivy at the far side of the pool.

Right In this carefully planned garden 'room' the formal structure of patio, lawn, path and border is softened by the mixed informal planting of the border and its collection of pots and urns. Backing the border, the pale scalloped fence, punctuated by pencil-thin columnar evergreens, sets off the pastel colours of the border plants and the green expanse of the lawn.

From here, the design opens out into three separate but connected areas, each formally laid out and symmetrical, but softened and enhanced by generous planting. A cool expanse of lawn is surrounded by a brick path and edged with two borders 6m/20ft long, each filled with flowers for both spring and summer display. The lawn then narrows and passes between two clipped box balls that mark the beginning of a circular area with a central pool. A semicircle of grass, a continuation of the lawn, wraps around one half of the pool, then the grass gives way to a brick path surrounded by more small balls of box. The pool is a mere 3cm/1½in. deep, but provides a beautifully calm light-reflecting surface that contrasts with the dark, shady area at the back of the garden.

In this final area, raised borders filled with camellias, azaleas and hydrangeas surround a circular brick terrace that makes a cool and secluded place to sit, restfully shaded by the arched canopy of a graceful oak. Hidden in a secret corner is a small path filled with ferns, swamp iris and the wild flowers of the countryside; known as 'Mrs Whaley's Lover's Lane', it comes as a last charming surprise.

Left Although the long borders also have summer displays, they are perhaps at their most charming in the pale colours of the South Carolina spring. Here, the white flowers of a camellia are matched by white stocks and by the delicate white pansies whose petals spill over the border, while the azalea with its deep pink throat finds an echo in the pink-splashed tulips.

Below left The classical urn, handsome lead whippet and basket-weave terracotta pot make a decorative display at the edge of the patio. The grouping has a charmingly informal air, but, for symmetry, is repeated at the other side of the garden. The two arrangements serve as sentinels to the curved edge of the lawn.

Below right The secluded circular brick terrace at the far end of the garden was designed to create the effect of a sunken area, and the heavy surrounding planting of azaleas, camellias and hydrangeas gives a feeling of woodland. Although the decorative blue-painted furniture matches that on the open patio near the house, the atmosphere and outlook of the two seating areas are quite different: this is a quiet, private place to sit.

A Patterned Garden

In the L-shaped garden of Mr and Mrs van Hoonacker, in the Belgian city of Bruges, the designer André van Wassenhove has constructed a contemporary version of the traditional parterre. Formal patterning can work very well in a small urban garden, and the straight boundary lines and flat featureless ground of this site were ideal starting points for an intricate design. However, while the conventional parterre is symmetrical, in this design hedging, paving, low brick walls and infill plants are combined in an asymmetrical layout that blends the traditional with the modern, and a feeling of intimacy with a sense of spaciousness.

Within the pattern height is provided by trees and shrubs, including an apple tree, a plum tree and a white mulberry (*Morus alba*), that break the strong horizontal plane of the box hedging and the low brick walls. In this shady garden, much of the planting has been chosen for foliage interest: conspicuous are several large plants of Boston ivy (*Parthenocissus tricuspidata*) that glow with colour in autumn.

Below left Box hedging provides a framework that contains infill plants, sheltering them in the growing season and contributing a presence in the winter, when they are dormant. Boston ivy (*Parthenocissus tricuspidata*), climbing over a low wall, contributes autumn colour.

Below right A small, raised square pool on the edge of the garden contains goldfish and water-loving plants. Surrounded by low walls, one draped with another plant of Boston ivy, the pool fits snugly into the rigidly right-angled layout. Ivy (*Hedera helix*) softens the appearance of the tall boundary wall behind.

Right The maze-like plan of this garden is based on rectangles, arranged in an assymmetrical pattern. Height is supplied by trees and shrubs such as the young white mulberry (*Morus alba*) and the pot-grown hydrangea and standard fuchsia.

A Tapestry of Times Past

Crook Hall is a magnificent Durham town house, medieval in origin and added to over several hundred years, with the main part of the building dating from the eighteenth century. The challenge of restoring the neglected garden of a venerable house may prompt an exercise in historical fidelity – an attempt at producing a garden that is meticulously faithful to the style of a particular period. But the result can seem sterile, more like a museum piece than a living garden. In the case of Crook Hall, where the house grew over several centuries, there was the additional difficulty of deciding which period to choose. Faced a decade ago with tackling Crook Hall's overgrown gardens (where couch grass and rose bay willow herb reigned supreme), John and Mary Hawgood decided against the imposition of any single historical 'style'. They chose to follow their instincts, rather than rigid rules, and have succeeded in creating a series of individual garden pictures that in different ways complement the dignity and complexity of the house.

The general air is one of informality. Part of the garden is surrounded by walls that offer vital shelter from the searing winds that tend to ravage plants in the north-east of England. These walls make a mellow backdrop to borders crowded, in cottage garden style, with quantities of old-fashioned roses and perennials – there are more than a hundred different species, to ensure a succession of flower colour. Countless bulbs have naturalized in wild areas where maintenance is kept to a minimum, and in informal grassy areas around the oldest part of the house, among the framework of mature trees the Hawgoods inherited. Here and there carefully chosen ornaments and sculptures punctuate the design, providing focal points.

To mark their silver wedding anniversary, the Hawgoods planted a silver and white garden. More recently, stimulated by a book about Shakespeare's flowers, Mary Hawgood has been establishing a Shakespeare garden that includes fifteen old roses, among them *Rosa centifolia*, *Rosa gallica* 'Versicolor' (Rosa Mundi) and *R. × alba* (the White Rose of York), annuals such as marigolds, larkspur and nasturtiums, and quantities of herbs. The centrepiece of this garden is an ancient urn that is to be framed by a pergola, the paths are paved with medieval flagstones and old bricks, and the beds will be edged with box and lavender. Such personal touches of 'history', like the old statues that people the garden, contribute to the atmosphere of maturity without making a dogmatic statement. The result is a garden in keeping with the spirit of a grand old house.

Left A narrow flagstone path leads through the wide borders of herbaceous perennials that weave a vivid summer tapestry in the front garden. In the choice of plants and the way they are informally massed this garden has a cottage garden style that is sympathetic to the mellow, domestic character of the house.

Below In this area blues and violets, reds, pinks and white blend in rich colour harmonies, making a picture that subtly changes from day to day. Lupin spikes and oriental poppies tower above dense mounds of blue and pink cranesbills, while quantities of pale pink and white night-scented sweet rocket and blue-spired veronicas edge the path.

A Green Haven

A dense green curtain surrounds this bosky garden, screening out the sights and sounds of central Paris. Tall horse chestnuts, field maples and false acacias around the perimeter make a leafy backdrop to lush naturalistic plantings that use the predominantly shady aspect to advantage.

The garden was designed by Gilles Clément – one of France's leading contemporary landscape architects – and it was he who, imaginatively, turned the conventional layout of central lawn and surrounding borders inside out, filling the centre of the garden with a mass of low shrubby planting and running meandering grassy paths around the edges. The island beds, which allow only glimpses across the garden, have the effect of making it appear larger than it really is.

Ground-covering plants suppress weeds, and keep maintenance to a minimum. In the largest bed, enriched with peaty soil, a group composed of *Parrotia persica*, *Nothofagus antarctica* and *Prunus serrula* is underplanted with heathers to give all-season interest. Next to the patio beside the house are beds of hybrid tea and floribunda roses with a ground cover of silvery-leaved *Cerastium tomentosum*. Nearby, *Cotoneaster lacteus* flourishes beside *Cornus florida*.

Rhododendrons and camellias benefit from the shade of the trees. Beneath them, ferns and acanthus provide dramatic foliage contrast, while the white flowers of sweet woodruff (*Galium odoratum*) and the yellow-green ones of *Euphorbia robbiae* lighten the darkest corners.

Below left The view from the house is framed by wrought-iron archways, softened by twining roses and vines. Beyond the paved terrace, winding grassy paths invite exploration of a jungle of shrubby greenery punctuated with seasonal flowers. In the sunniest spot beds of hybrid tea and floribunda roses make a bright scented splash throughout the summer. They are underplanted with the grey-foliaged *Cerastium tomentosum*. The transition from patio area to garden is marked by a loosely shaped mound of box that sounds a muted note of formality before more relaxed planting takes over.

Right The backdrop of trees creates an atmosphere of tranquillity in this Parisian garden. Against the wisteria-draped house a spacious terrace accommodates the civilized pleasures of outdoor eating and drinking; the sinuous lines of the patio furniture echo the curves of the ironwork pergola and the looping branches of the fig tree overhead. Both the terrace and the adjacent rose beds benefit from being bathed in sun during the morning. Beside the regular slabs of the terrace, a crazy paving path leads into the leafy wilderness.

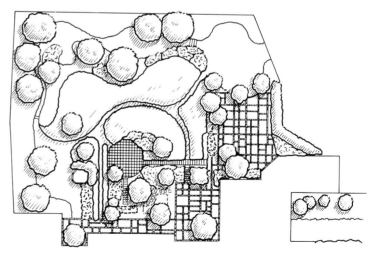

A GARDEN FOR ENTERTAINING

Stewart and Jackie McColl have turned their small London garden into an elegant conversation piece that makes witty allusions to nearby Regent's Park. The McColls run a busy architecture and design practice, and they wanted a garden they could use for entertaining. The garden they have created, with the help of landscape consultant Anthony Paul, shows how much can be achieved in a shaded space only 20m/65ft long by 10m/33ft wide.

It was a bold decision to devote so much of this space to a pond that spans the garden, dividing it in two. Mirrored arches at either end of the pool make the garden look wider – and also, in a joking allusion to Regent's Park Canal, create the impression that the water flows through the garden. Beyond the pool lies the garden's focal point, a summerhouse modelled after the Chinese-style tea-house in the Park. At night skilled lighting (shown on page 19) brings a magical scene to life.

Two mature trees – a lime, *Tilia cordata*, and an ornamental cherry, *Prunus cerasus* – contribute a vertical element to the garden and increase privacy, but also limit the choice of plants to those that thrive in shade. Bold evergreen *Fatsia japonica* and large-leaved ivies were chosen to form a strong background and ensure that the garden is green throughout the year. *Mahonia japonica* contributes colour and scent in winter and spring; the crimson blooms of miniature roses and the fluffy pink panicles of *Rodgersia pinnata* bring summer colour, and autumn turns the Japanese maples fiery red.

Below left Water rising from a fountain set in a scalloped stone bowl is reflected in the mirrored arches at either end of the pool. On the pool's edge the bold foliage of a bergenia contrasts with the delicate leaves of an acer in a black Chinese pot.

Below right An elegant Chinese-style bridge leads to the shady enclave at the far side of the garden. Graceful maples arch over the water's edge.

Right On the far side of the pool, a handsome summerhouse, modelled on the tea-house in Regent's Park, is a striking focal point, and also a pleasant, secluded place to sit and contemplate the garden. A combination of mellow bricks and good-quality stone flags makes an attractive and practical all-weather surface.

JAPANESE INSPIRATION

Mr and Mrs Allan Lee, who own this garden, have a long-established interest in Japan. When, in 1963, they were planning to make a garden for their house in Hillsborough, near San Francisco, they decided that they wanted their garden to have the serenity and subtle symbolism of the traditional Japanese garden, and also to provide an appropriate setting for their remarkable collection of ancient Japanese trees and garden ornaments. They asked Nagao Sakurai, a well-known Japanese landscape architect, to design a garden for them.

The area behind the house, a broad, shallow rectangle in plan, was originally a featureless flat lawn, exposed to neighbouring gardens. A hedge of dense mixed planting was established along the boundary, to provide privacy while retaining distant views. Then in one corner of the garden a gently sloping earth mound was constructed and heavily planted, to suggest a hilly, forested terrain. These trees and shrubs blend imperceptibly into the boundary hedge and the mature trees in the middle distance: the garden's boundary is blurred and scenery beyond the garden 'borrowed' to create the impression of an expanse of woodland. The tiny 'mountain' also provides the setting for a stream that cascades down in a rushing waterfall, then flows into a curving pool below.

As is traditional in Japan, the garden is for viewing from inside or immediately outside the house, rather than for active use. Also in keeping with tradition is the smooth transition from house to garden: plants near the house have been clipped into semi-architectural forms; sliding glass doors and glass walls open from the house on to the garden; and a small courtyard is surrounded on three sides by the glass walls of the house and opens on the fourth side on to the garden. To create a sense of unity, restraint and rhythm, a limited range of species is used repeatedly: Japanese maples, pines, junipers, magnolias, rhododendrons, azaleas and elaeagnus, all carefully clipped or pruned. Above all, a Japanese garden is intended to encourage the contemplation of nature; an aim in which this American city garden admirably succeeds.

Every view in a Japanese garden is carefully conceived, and viewing points, or viewing stones, are set out to assist in the enjoyment and appreciation of the garden. Here the main axis, taking in the stream, the waterfall and the densely planted hill, is designed to be seen through the glass wall of the living room and, outdoors, from the adjacent stone veranda. The view crosses the garden diagonally, to maximize the sense of depth and spaciousness, and to take full advantage of the 'borrowed' landscape of mature trees beyond. Garden ornaments on this main axis include a pair of bronze cranes, the Japanese symbol of the universal masculine, conquering element, or *yang*; a traditional 'tortoise island', symbolizing the universal feminine, earthbound element, *yin*; and two stone lanterns.

Above The focal point of the courtyard is a large Hinoki cypress (*Chamaecyparis obtusa*), one of two owned by the Lees. These trees, 750 years old, were given by the Japanese government to the 1915 Panama Pacific Exposition. Their containers are Tzu Chou tubs of the sixth century AD. The undulating ground cover was inspired by the moss garden of the Kyoto Saiho-ji temple, though, in this dry garden, the moss has been replaced by sagina and helxine.

Right In the courtyard, a stone lantern nestles against a horizontal juniper, with, nearby, clumps of lily turf, or liriope, and Japanese azaleas that have been clipped to resemble smooth, round stones. The cobbles help to link the house and garden visually, and they provide a practical and beautiful surface for the dry, shady ground under the eaves, where few plants could survive. Folding rice paper screens, or *shoji*, behind the wall of glass, can be adjusted to define the view.

A PLANT LOVER'S GARDEN

In 1974, when Lucy Gent and her husband, Malcolm Turner, moved into their eighteenth-century terraced house in London, the space behind the house was little more than a neglected and deeply shaded back yard. She has transformed it into a garden of impressive fullness and maturity, and a paradise for the plant lover.

This garden is 40m/125ft long and only 5m/16ft wide. High walls, built originally to provide privacy, both shade the site and make it seem even narrower. Moreover, the garden also contains two substantial trees: a large evergreen yew and a gnarled and ancient pyracantha. A more reckless gardener might have been tempted to cut down the trees to let in some sunlight, but Lucy Gent, recognizing their value as focal points, chose instead to integrate them into her plan.

Although the design of the garden could hardly be simpler, the density of the planting ensures that the eye is continually distracted, and scarcely registers the long, narrow shape. The main path is set off-centre to make the most of the growing

Below left Near the bench that has been positioned a third of the way down the garden, dark-leaved *Heuchera* 'Palace Purple' spills from a black pot, while pink *Francoa ramosa*, orange *Lilium henryi*, blue *Aconitum* 'Bressingham Spire' and pink-red *Fuchsia* 'Thalia' form a medley of colour among varying foliage.

Right The view from the upper windows of the house reveals the simple linear plan of the garden. Two beautiful black-glazed pots by Jeny Jones, one planted with honeysuckle, the other with *Heuchera* 'Palace Purple' make telling focal points.

The planting includes:

1 TREES AND SHRUBS: *Camellia* 'Cornish Snow', *C.* 'Nuccio's Gem', *Daphne pontica, Hamamelis × intermedia* 'Carmine Red', *Hydrangea aspera villosa, H. sargentiana, Prunus × subhirtella* 'Autumnalis', *Rhododendron yakushimanum, Skimmia japonica, Taxus baccata, Viburnum × bodnantense* 'Dawn', *V. davidii.*
CLIMBING PLANTS: *Clematis armandii, C.* 'Jackmanii Alba', *Rosa* 'Madame Alfred Carrière' *Schizophragma integrifolium.*
PERENNIALS: *Cimicifuga racemosa, Epimedium × versicolor* 'Sulphureum', *Helleborus × sternii, Hosta sieboldiana, Matteuccia struthiopteris, Polygonatum × hybridum* 'Flore Pleno'.

2 TREES AND SHRUBS: *Camellia* 'Leonard Messel', *Carpenteria californica, Ceanothus* 'Autumnal Blue', *Corylopsis pauciflora, Gleditsia triacanthos* 'Ruby Lace', *Sarcococca confusa, Sorbus hupehensis obtusa.*
CLIMBING PLANTS: *Clematis* 'Etoile Rose', *C. macropetala, C. × durandii, Rosa* 'New Dawn'.
PERENNIALS: *Aconitum* 'Bressingham Spire', *Allium cernuum, Astrantia carniolica rubra, Bergenia* 'Abendglut', *Dicentra* 'Langtrees', *Geranium wallichianum* 'Buxton's Variety', *Helleborus lividus, Heuchera* 'Palace Purple', *Paeonia mlokosewitschii*

3 TREES AND SHRUBS: *Ceanothus* 'Southmead', *Elaeagnus × ebbingei, Magnolia stellata, Myrtus luma, Phlomis fruticosa, Pyracantha coccinea, Rosa glauca, R. moyesii, R.* 'Margaret Merril', *R.* 'Nevada', *Styrax japonica.*
CLIMBING PLANTS: *Clematis* 'Niobe', *C. viticella* 'Rubra', *C.* 'Marie Boisselot', *Rosa* 'Zéphirine Drouhin', *R.* 'Albertine'.
PERENNIALS: *Acanthus mollis, Alstroemeria* Ligtu Hybrids, *Campanula alliarifolia, Rudbeckia* 'Herbstsonne'.

4 TREES AND SHRUBS: *Abelia × grandiflora, Buddleja fallowiana* 'Alba', *Cercidiphyllum japonicum, Chimonanthus praecox, Corokia × virgata, Daphne odora, Enkianthus campanulatus, Eucryphia × intermedia, Paeonia suffruticosa, Rosa rugosa* 'Blanc Double de Coubert', *Rubus* Tridel 'Benenden', *Viburnum rhytidophyllum.*
CLIMBING PLANTS: *Clematis alpina* 'Columbine', *Rosa* 'Paul's Lemon Pillar', *R.* 'Guinée', *Vitis vinifera* 'Purpurea'.
PERENNIAL: *Chrysanthemum* 'Emperor of China'.

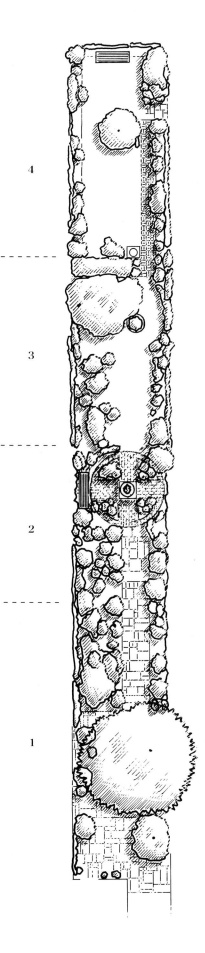

Left Lucy Gent has described this garden as a chemistry lab, in which she is always trying out new combinations. In the inspired grouping shown here the strap-shaped leaves of the lemon-yellow lily 'La Bohème' are echoed in the feathery fronds of the ostrich fern, *Matteuccia struthiopteris*, while a stray seedling of blue *Campanula persicifolia* thrusts its stem through the purplish florets of *Hydrangea aspera villosa*.

Right In this garden every tiny space is richly planted. Between the bench and large-leaved *Paeonia mlokosewitschii* stands a terracotta pot filled with *Helichrysum petiolare*, with its creamy flowers and felty green leaves, underplanted with variegated *Felicia amelloides*.

space on the sunnier side of the garden. The beds on both sides are packed with plants. Aiming at an effect of exuberant lushness, and recognizing that frost and the shady conditions would see off some of her more daring choices, Lucy Gent decided at the outset to overplant. Occasionally she has had to remove a shrub that proved too vigorous, but she is usually able to maintain a balance by judicious pruning.

Full use has been made of all the available growing space. The long, tall boundary walls, further heightened by trellis, are clothed with an abundance of climbers. Conspicuous among the shrubs on the shady wall is the lovely *Schizophragma integrifolium*: a wonderful climber for shady conditions, it produces masses of large white inflorescences over a long flowering season. On the sunnier wall opposite, roses and clematis combine to give a succession of blooms. *Clematis armandii*, with its profuse and scented waxy-white blooms, is the first to flower. As its petals drop, the first buds of *Clematis* 'Jackmanii Alba' are beginning to open. In June the lovely old rose 'Madame Alfred Carrière' takes over, and, with regular deadheading, it continues to put out its crisp white scented flowers all summer.

The beds below are planted with a mixture of shrubs and perennials that tend to fall into groups in which there is a play between foliage size and colour; in this way contrast and variety are built up in the interweaving tapestry of leaves that runs the length of the garden. For example, one group combines small-leaved *Corokia* × *virgata*, peonies with their large cut leaves and *Rubus* Tridel 'Benenden', a shrub with felted white undersides to its leaves. The path edges are lined by plants of varying heights: sometimes low-growing ground-cover plants, such as hostas and geraniums, sometimes the taller ostrich fern (*Matteuccia struthiopteris*) or fragrant *Daphne odora*.

About a third of the way down the garden, a south-facing bench offers an invitation to pause and contemplate the scene. The position was chosen to make the best of a view of an ancient pear tree in a neighbour's garden. Plants that flower earlier than the rest have been grouped around this bench, so that in spring it is surrounded by the marbled leaves and greenish-pink blooms of *Helleborus* × *sternii* and the snowy blossoms of *Amelanchier canadensis* and white camellias.

Another seat has been placed at the end of the garden, to provide a long backward view to the house. Turning around, the observer sees the garden from a fresh perspective and, after a brief rest, will surely want to begin exploring again.

A GARDEN OF SYMBOLISM

The apparent simplicity of this unusual garden is deceptive: it is, in fact, highly complex, with every feature planned to have an overtly symbolic content. Set in the middle of London, the garden was conceived and planned five years ago by the owners, Charles Jencks, doyen of architectural symbolism, and his wife, Maggie Keswick, who has written the definitive book on Chinese gardens. It is based on a strong symmetrical layout. A spacious central lawn is bounded by a waist-high yew hedge which leads the eye to a pavilion; around the periphery runs a path, and it is here that the symbolism is revealed. Each of the four corners represents a point on the compass, and one circuit a journey both around the world and through a year. Thus the east corner is China and the spring, the south is Egypt and summer, the west is the United States and autumn, and the north is Europe and winter. The planting echoes the characteristic colours of the seasons, and the plants and ornaments originate from the regions represented – for example, there are pots from China, a paulownia from Egypt. The themes have been planned to work together both visually and intellectually, making a garden that appeals on many levels.

Below left One of the side boundaries of the garden, showing six mirrored doors that serve the design on a practical level, making the garden appear larger, reflecting more light into it, and – because they are placed exactly opposite six more on the other side – emphasizing the cross axes. As well, they symbolize both the months of the year and openings into different worlds. The international telephone dialling codes for twelve cultural capitals are to be inscribed in stone along the paths, to allude to the ease with which the world's different cultures can now communicate.

Below right The Future Pavilion, so called because inscribed on its door is the epithet 'The Future is Behind You' – a reference to the architecture of the house, which is reflected in the mirror. Built on converging lines, the pavilion accentuates the perspective, increasing the illusion of depth and space. The concept of symmetry is so important to the owners that there are even two handles on the door.

Right The symmetry of the garden is best appreciated from the two windows on the upper floor of the house, which roll down at the touch of a button, giving the impression that already one is almost in the garden. From here a double staircase leads down. The main vista, its length optically increased by the mirrored door, is to the Future Pavilion.

A WOODLAND GARDEN

The couple who own this leafy retreat, in the densely built-up Saint Germain-des-Prés district of Paris, started with very different visions of the ideal garden. He wanted to be reminded of the sunny Mediterranean, she of the mysterious forests of Germany, where she grew up. Remarkably, landscape architect Ulrike Klages succeeded in designing a garden that delights them both.

The plan of the garden is simple: a paved area alongside the house provides a tranquil spot to relax in after a day's work. From here a path traces a serpentine way through island beds whose lush foliage conceals the boundaries of the garden, creating the illusion that it extends well beyond its actual limits.

The south-facing orientation helped to clarify the planting scheme. On the terrace beside the house, which gets most of the sun, palm trees that are hardy enough to withstand the occasional light frost evoke the boulevards of the Mediterranean. Free-flowering *Nerium oleander*, a distinctive shrub of hot, dry regions, is grown in large terracotta tubs that can be moved indoors for winter protection. Fruit-bearing figs soften the harshness of the yellow brick walls.

Further down the garden high walls provide shade for woodland shrubs: azaleas, rhododendrons, magnolias and *Camellia japonica* 'Alba Plena'. Quantities of leafmould, mixed with grit, were dug into the alkaline soil to provide the acidic moisture-retentive medium that these plants need in order to thrive.

The underplanting was carefully chosen to ensure a long flowering season. The Christmas rose (*Helleborus niger*) is the first to flower, followed by masses of daffodils and tulips. The shrubs themselves burst into one concerted mass of blooms in early summer. Bedding plants such as pelargoniums and impatiens, grouped informally, flower through much of the summer, alongside the tall plumes of astilbes.

In this garden all the flowers are white. Green and white, the owner contends, is the most relaxing colour combination, and within these two colours there is such an abundance of subtle shades that she is never bored by her self-imposed restriction.

Left Tender plants evocative of the Mediterranean thrive in the sunny area close to the house. Date palms (*Phoenix* species) have been planted in containers to restrict their growth; nearby, the graceful leaves of the fan palm (*Chamaerops humilis*) rise from its fibre-covered trunk. Bamboo (*Arundinaria japonica*) fills an awkward corner, and *Wisteria sinensis* graces the stonework. Mat-forming helxine has been used as ground cover.

Right Densely planted with evergreen shrubs – rhododendrons, azaleas, camellias, pieris – this corner of the garden evokes the shady secrecy of a woodland glade. A slender glasshouse, against the brick wall, shelters more tender plants. The wall is clothed by a glory vine (*Vitis coignetiae*) that in the autumn will glow in different shades of crimson.

A Timeless Courtyard

This quiet Californian courtyard and the six adjoining studios that surround it have a timeless appeal. The brick paving of the courtyard, laid in a basket-weave pattern, is reminiscent of the tiles of Moorish courtyard gardens, while the simple stucco façades of the studios draw on Spanish missionary architecture, and have been painted, using a sponging technique, to look weathered by the ages.

In plan the courtyard is a double diamond, its sides formed by the staggered walls of the three studios on either side. This double diamond layout, with its narrow interconnecting neck, makes a space that is more interesting, and more intimate, than one large square or diamond, and allows the planting beds that hug the walls to assume attractively fluid shapes.

In this sheltered garden in a frost-free climate, half-hardy and tender plants, including pelargoniums, bougainvillea and hibiscus, thrive. Large trees, among them a great evergreen elm with a trunk that is beautifully sculptured, angled and forked, provide shade and a vertical element. In spring the garden is dominated by an ancient wisteria (shown on page 34), whose mauve blooms inspired the colouring of the walls.

Right An evergreen elm (*Ulmus parviflora*), its patchy bark contributing to the painterly quality of the scene, forms a focal point. A grape vine covers one wall, providing shade and fruit in summer, and attractive pale stems in winter. Flower-filled hanging baskets and a potted rubber plant add a personal, welcoming touch to a private doorway.

Below A stone putto, grasping a bunch of stone grapes in one hand and a wine flagon in the other, overlooks the garden. Thick-stemmed climbers, ferns, shrubby hibiscus and a multi-stemmed loquat grow in the dappled shade.

A Garden Romance

Behind the high, ivy-clad wall that conceals her front garden from the London street, Mrs Barclay has transformed a rectangular plot into a country house garden in miniature. A cleverly conceived blend of formal and informal planting with paving and stonework belies the relatively small space, creating an atmosphere of romance and abundance.

The entrance is framed by an arch that is almost hidden beneath the gold-variegated ivy 'Goldheart'. A second archway, its tracery more visible among twining roses, leads from the main path towards the neat central parterre that forms the focal point of the garden. Here a double edging of box and *Lonicera nitida* 'Baggesen's Gold' ties together a quincunx of clipped box spirals. The strong green structure of this topiary, satisfyingly solid although slightly whimsical, tempers the cottage garden profusion of the surrounding borders.

All around this garden are beds with a variety of shrubs and herbaceous plants to ensure all-year interest and a succession of delightful associations. Viburnums, choisya, mahonia, *Daphne odora* and *Rhododendron* Cilpinense all flourish, with *Pittosporum tenuifolium* 'Variegatum', *Euonymus fortunei radicans* 'Variegatum', *Berberis thunbergii* 'Rose Glow' and *Pyrus salicifolia* providing contrast of leaf colour. Climbers scramble upwards, clothing the house and the garden walls, while clematis and *Garrya elliptica* respectively enwrap the pair of recumbent horses that flank the entrance steps. A small pool is almost hidden in one corner.

Mrs Barclay has a strong belief in the effectiveness of bold plants in small spaces. Among colours, she particularly likes to combine pale yellow and purple, and enjoys the effect of a lemon-yellow daffodil with a dark form of hellebore, and of *Erysimum* 'Bowles' Mauve' with *Euphorbia characias wulfenii*.

There is, of course, variation from season to season: for example, depending on the time of year, the bedding in the parterre, beneath the two standard 'The Fairy' roses, might be green and white tulips, a mass of white antirrhinums, a blend of santolina and lavender, or the camomile lawn of a sixteenth-century knot. More radical changes are undertaken as soon as Mrs Barclay's instinct tells her something is out of balance. Both this front garden and the courtyard behind the house are single-compartment gardens, where the whole area must look good all year round, and Mrs Barclay is insistent that every plant must work hard for its space. Each one must make the desired contribution to the design, and they must all thrive and look happy. Any that fail, in any of these respects, are removed ruthlessly.

Left A blend of formal planting, paving, climber-clad walls and herbaceous borders conjures the romance of a country house garden beside a London street. The parterre with its twin hedges – a dark frame of box and a lighter inner edging of *Lonicera nitida* 'Baggesen's Gold' – establishes a firm structure, punctuated by the five spirals in clipped box.

Below Rose 'New Dawn' and *Hedera helix* 'Goldheart', climbing over the stucco gateposts of the entrance, draw the eye into the garden. The combination of evergreen foliage with luxuriant flowers sets the keynote for this garden. *Alchemilla mollis*, hellebores, lavender and campanulas, spilling over the path edge, hint at further riches within.

Mrs Barclay exercises the same discrimination, constantly grooming and adjusting each composition, in her second garden – a courtyard bounded on three sides by the house and on the fourth by a high brick wall. On one side is a conservatory, with glass doors that are often left open, blurring the distinction between indoors and out. The use of tile flooring in both conservatory and courtyard emphasizes this continuity.

In this small space the vertical dimension is exploited to the full. The walls are covered in climbers, including ivies in variety, Virginia creeper (*Parthenocissus quinquefolia*), clematis and roses. An espaliered peach tree fruits annually, high up, where the light intensity is sufficiently strong. A golden false acacia (*Robinia pseudoacacia* 'Frisia') hugs the brick wall, adding a little extra height. The only growing space is in a few narrow raised beds, so pots – in all shapes, sizes and patterns, though mostly of terracotta – play a vital role in the composition. Smaller plants include begonias, impatiens, ferns, euonymus, hostas and hellebores, all of which tolerate shade.

Sculpture is skilfully deployed: busts and statues, plaques and masks act as focal points and complete each individual composition, peopling the greenery with objects for contemplation, in the classical tradition. However, they are placed so that they are witty rather than pompous.

Trompe-l'oeil trickery of trellis and mirrors on the exterior walls is used subtly, subdued by greenery, to add another dimension to the tiny space; and mirrors have also been carefully placed in the ground floor rooms to reflect the views and bring the garden into the house.

Left A tiled floor creates a cool setting for this richly planted courtyard: the 15cm/6in. black-and-white tiles are set diagonally, expanding the boundaries of the tiny space. Mellow clay pots of plants, including an unusual pink shrubby mallow and a pot pyramid of herbs, stand out against the foliage of the wall planting – ivies, a camellia, a rose and *Clematis* 'Marie Boisselot'. The shady raised borders are lightened by variegated hostas and euonymus, and a white impatiens. The weathered statue and the handsome garden furniture contribute to the restful atmosphere.

Right In another corner of the courtyard a rich mixture of shade-loving plants makes a tapestry of leaf textures. Climbers include Virginia creeper and two variegated ivies; camellias, hostas, ferns, begonias, ballota, the spiky dark cordyline and variegated *Yucca gloriosa* provide further contrast of leaf forms. All are carefully arranged to complement the sculpture that forms the dramatic focal point of the court.

A Luxuriant Balcony

Left Plexiglass panels provide a protective backing for an abundant array of plants, including a blue potato vine (*Solanum crispum*), blue and white *Agapanthus praecox orientalis*, an oleander, *Hebe* 'Veronica Lake', mint and other herbs, and red salvia. *Bougainvillea* 'San Diego Red' cuts a swathe of colour across the trellis opposite, while red-splashed white petunias, dark blue lobelia, more herbs, orange-red nasturtiums and a terracotta cherub thrive in the decorative pots below. At the shady end of the balcony a tree form of *Ligustrum japonicum* flourishes, and behind it *Hardenbergia comptoniana* and evergreen jasmine twine through the lattice.

This secluded balcony garden, in the middle of busy San Francisco, was devised to provide an outdoor dining room for the owner, psychiatrist David Leof – and to satisfy his longing for an 'illusion of Tuscany'. It measures only 3 × 6m/10 × 20ft but, because it is on an upper floor, it receives enough light for a multitude of plants to flourish. As David Leof says, he almost has to 'brush aside the greenery to get to the table'.

The first concern of the designer, Josephine Zeitlin, was to combat the chilly sea breezes that blow off the bay. To protect both diners and the less hardy plants, three plexiglass panels (lighter and safer than sheets of glass) were installed along one side of the balcony. Sturdy trellis has been run along the other two sides, for increased privacy and to support climbing plants.

Year-round screening is maintained by a backdrop of hardy, mainly broad-leaved evergreen plants in Italian terracotta pots. Plants including a bougainvillea, nasturtiums, lilies, lobelia, petunias, salvias and aromatic herbs have been added for richness, colour and scent. All have been chosen to harmonize: there are no violent contrasts, and variations are soft and subtle. The atmosphere is one of luxuriant calm.

Right The view from the french windows of the kitchen is an invitation to dine in the hazy sunshine outside, protected from both prying eyes and cool sea breezes. Plants of subtly varying leaf shape and texture make evergreen screens that are never without an enlivening touch of colour – in the microclimate provided by the plexiglass panels, even plants as tender as nasturtiums bloom throughout the winter.

A Geometric Garden

Above From the timber decking next to the house the eye is directed along the stepping stone and pebble path down to the end of the garden. The view is framed by two rounded mounds of box planted in terracotta pots, and *Alchemilla mollis* spills from beds, blurring the edges of the path. There are spots of pale colour: the white of *Hydrangea petiolaris* on the dark fence matches *Lamium* 'White Nancy' in the near beds; foxgloves in the distance echo the red of *Hydrangea sargentiana* in the corner of the middle terrace; and the hazy pink of *Geranium endressii* brightens the far terrace.

Right An informal collection of decorative terracotta pots creates a tiny herb garden in the corner of the terrace nearest the house. The clear lines of the beds, paths, pools and terraces are softened by the rounded forms of alchemilla and hostas and the arching shapes of ornamental grasses such as *Luzula nivea*.

The garden owned and designed by Piet Oudolf, in De Hummelo, Holland, is open and light in feeling. Because of the clear patterns of its geometric shapes it looks as effective from the upper storeys of the house as it does from ground level. The plot is asymmetric – long and tapering – and a narrow path winds around the edge. Inside, a strict formality is displayed in severely rectilinear shapes – squares and long, thin oblongs. However, the planting softens the design: plants such as geraniums, *Alchemilla mollis*, lamiums and ornamental grasses, with their rounded or arching forms, spill freely over the edges of their beds; even the hedges are not tightly clipped.

A stepping stone path of paving slabs and pebbles creates a strong axis slightly to one side of the plot, firmly leading the eye to the far end, where a large open terrace gives a feeling of space to this narrowest part of the garden. Paved strips, beds and three canal-like pools of water create a series of horizontal lines across the garden, giving some breadth to the long plot. The rectangular shapes of terraces contribute solidity, while the reflective pools lighten the whole design.

The prevailing colour scheme is in soft shades of green, accented here and there with flowers of white and paler pastel colours – *Hydrangea petiolaris, Anemone × hybrida* 'Honorine Jobert', *Geranium endressii, Lamium* 'White Nancy'. The planting as a whole is fairly low-growing, in keeping with the open, level feeling of the garden. However, taller elements are used, sparingly but effectively, to add height. The central feature is a graceful crab apple that arches over the garden. Three thin-sparred obelisks placed at the corners of the end terrace, as support for climbers, have an architectural effect. And at middle height are grasses and foxgloves, and hedges of beech.

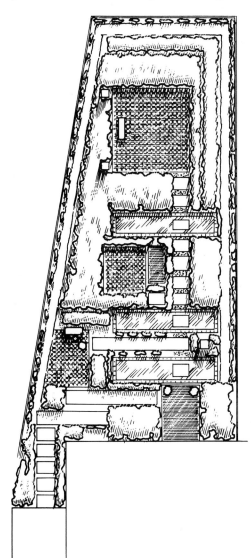

A LEAFY OASIS

This tiny garden, situated near the centre of Milan, provides a quiet haven away from the bustle of the city. The garden has a firm focus in the centrally placed stone fountain and pool; otherwise the design is free and informal, as is the planting. The overall impression is of a calm, leafy greenness, with the trickling water from the fountain cooling and refreshing the atmosphere and apple and lime trees offering welcome shade.

Next to the house is a terrace, part shaded and part in sun, much used in the summer for relaxing, dining and entertaining. It is paved with porphyry setts laid in circular patterns, and is decorated with plants in attractive terracotta pots.

The main garden is a sun-dappled lawn: in spring the grass is left to grow long, and a charming profusion of white daisies lightens its lush green. A mown grass path winds through the lawn, curving from the terrace around the fountain to the bottom of the garden, where it ends at a pergola smothered with the pale yellow flowers of *Rosa banksiae* 'Lutescens'.

Below left Groups of plants in terracotta pots decorate the paved terrace next to the house. Near the entrance a large *Loropetalum chinense*, a shrub that is hardy only in warm gardens, flowers abundantly.

Below The handsome stone fountain with its tranquil pool and sparkling jets of water makes an arresting centrepiece for the garden. Its solid formality is softened by moss growing on the plinth and the greenery spilling over the edges of the pool. The surrounding grass is scattered with daisies, and, behind, a pergola covered with *Rosa banksiae* 'Lutescens' brightens the end of the garden.

Right With its table and chairs and shady umbrella, the paved terrace outside the house provides a pleasant place to sit for an outdoor meal, or just to relax and enjoy the garden.

A Paradise Garden

This long, narrow city garden, belonging to the landscape architect Richard Tan, shows what possibilities may lie within a thin strip of land. The owner-designer wanted to create a tropical paradise that would serve as a retreat from the busy city life of Singapore. The obstacles in his way included, as well as the uninteresting shape of the plot, those other familiar problems of urban gardening: limited space, and lack of privacy, because of the close proximity of neighbours.

The central position of the house divides the site into three. The front contains a lawn, a terrace and car parking space; the middle section is largely taken up by the house, but has to one side a long, thin corridor of garden that links the front and back, and on the other a small, rectangular garden room; and the small back garden is a lawn surrounded by planting.

The garden begins in the street outside: planted in a narrow strip next to the pavement, a huge *Cassia fistula*, with its yellow, lantern-like blooms, welcomes the visitor and forms a backdrop for the front garden as it is seen from the house. Borders, densely planted for screening, completely surround the garden. For much of their course these borders are straight and narrow, but they are widened, to form generously curving beds, in key places: on either side of a short flight of steps that leads from the car parking area to the lawn; at the approach from the front to the side garden, to surround a tiny pond crossed by stepping stones; and where the side garden opens out into the back garden. These 'bottlenecks' of abundant greenery make the lawn seem more expansive by comparison, and contribute to a sense of seclusion.

Left A dining area in the side garden, with easy access, by french windows, from the living room, dining room and kitchen, offers a perfect setting for meals outdoors. The raised wooden decking provides a dry, level surface underfoot. Densely planted palms, underplanted with the painted drop tongue (*Aglaonema* 'Gayle') and dumb cane (*Dieffenbachia* species), screen the garden from onlookers.

Right A dark pond, crossed by irregularly shaped stepping stones and overhung with lush tropical foliage, divides the front and side gardens. Though the pond is tiny, to fit the small space available, it makes an effective focal point. A sense of movement is created by the changing reflections of the sky, the activity of the koi carp, and the way the small fountain ripples the pond's surface. The splashing of the water from the fountain also contributes a soothing background sound that masks some of the city's noise.

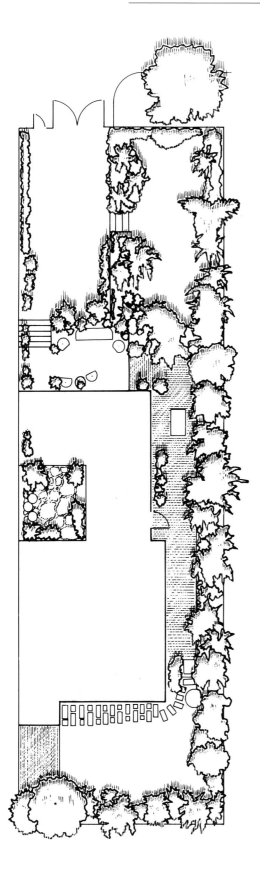

Tender plants that are cosseted indoors in temperate countries grow luxuriously in the tropical climate of Singapore, and this garden has a jungly lushness. More than twenty species of palm, including the yellow, or areca, palm (*Chrysalidocarpus lutescens*), the lady palm (*Rhapis excelsa*) and the miniature date palm (*Phoenix roebelenii*) form the backbone of the planting. Their richly textured, upright trunks make them ideal trees for a small space, and the graceful fronds create overhead shade and seclusion. The sealing wax palm, *Cyrtostachys lakka*, with its dense thickets of bamboo-like stems, is especially valuable for screening.

The back garden was planned to be functional, as well as attractive, and it provides many ingredients for the kitchen. There are fruit trees – limes, oranges and *Achras sapota*, the marmalade plum, with its sweet, russet-brown, scented fruit; and herbs and spices, including chili, lemon grass and ginger.

Finally, to complete the illusion of paradise, tropical birds, butterflies and tiny squirrels, drawn by the flowers and fruit, have made the garden their home.

Left Where space allows, curving beds soften the straight lines of the lawn and boundaries. Here a pair of squat cycas palms (*Cycas revoluta*) forms the central feature in a densely planted bed of coral and pink *Ixora chinensis* and spathiphyllum, with variegated dracaena in the foreground. Also called sago or fern palm, the cycas palm is not a true palm, but a slow-growing member of the Cycadaceae family, related to conifers, and one of the most primitive flowering plants. In temperate climates it is grown in conservatories for its rosette of ferny leaves; these are also much sought after by flower arrangers, especially for use in dried flower displays. The plant's curious, brown-felted, pineapple-like base serves as a water reserve in times of drought.

Right The narrow corridor of the side garden creates a tunnel for breezes; and seen from the front garden, the dining area on the raised decking looks cool, shady and inviting. Tell-tale signs of civilization in this jungle garden include the light fixture near the pond, to ensure a safe passage across the water at night; and the small stone statue, tucked under the fronds of bird's nest fern (*Asplenium nidus*), and surrounded by African daisies (*Arctotis* species) and the colourful foliage of angels' wings (*Caladium* species). In the opposite bed, the sword-like leaves of screw pine (*Pandanus veitchii*) rise from a ground cover of boat lily (*Rhoeo* 'Tricolor Dwarf'), interspersed with clumps of ferns.

A CONSERVATORY GARDEN

Recently restored to its original Edwardian splendour, the spacious south-facing conservatory of this London house makes feasible a more exotic garden than could otherwise be achieved in the British climate. Decorative, and ideal for entertaining, it serves to extend the summer, and enables the owners to cultivate plants that could not survive without protection.

Marcus and Pen Linell, who have owned the house for twelve years, do not have constant heating in the conservatory – just two thermostatically controlled fan heaters that they turn on when it becomes too cool for comfort – but this has not prevented them from growing an interesting collection of plants that includes citrus trees and a climbing blue *Plumbago auriculata*. The *pièce de résistance* is a grape vine planted by previous owners, some twenty-five years ago. Its framework of

bare stems lets in light in winter, but in full summer leaf it provides just the right amount of shade; and the work involved in pruning it in summer and winter, and watering it during the summer, is amply rewarded by a plentiful crop of fruit.

The Linells chose for the conservatory traditional cane furniture, which is in keeping with the character and age of the building and, while being more comfortable than wood or metal alternatives, still has a garden atmosphere.

The conservatory and the sitting room open on to a paved terrace. Here, to make sure there are always flowers to enjoy, the evergreen shrubs in the narrow beds are augmented by a varying array of flowering potted plants, each of which plays its part during the year. So, for example, the daffodils and tulips of spring are replaced by lilies and daisies in the summer.

Left Paved in York stone, and furnished with elegant modern chairs and table, the east-facing corner of the terrace is an ideal place for summer meals: a sun trap at breakfast and a shady spot for the middle of the day. *Wisteria floribunda* 'Alba' climbs up around the windows, and a succession of terracotta pots provides a changing display of flowers.

Right Blue *Plumbago auriculata* and clear yellow abutilon mingle delightfully as they climb the conservatory wall (also shown on page 30). Lilies, geraniums and citrus trees, some planted in handsome Chinese pots, others in less exotic containers concealed by white *cache-pots*, are arranged on the floor, while smaller pots are raised to eye level on a Victorian cast-iron stand. The quarry tile floor is easy to clean, and doesn't mind getting wet when the plants are watered. The original iron heating grate on the floor is no longer in use, but has been retained for its decorative appeal.

A GARDEN OF ILLUSION

Nan McEvoy knew clearly that what she wanted in the tiny space behind her nineteenth-century house in Georgetown, Washington D.C., was a classical formal garden that would also serve her practical needs. The site was a difficult one: measuring just 15 × 9m/50 × 30ft, it sloped both from east to west and from north to south. Mrs McEvoy wanted the garden to look cool, green and timeless, to have a strong structure, so that she could change the planting without affecting the basic design, and to include raised beds for easy maintenance, water, so that she could swim, and a position for a favourite statue.

The garden created for her by landscape architect David Campbell is a masterpiece of illusion. She looks out from her windows on a quiet scene of green grass and deep, limpid water, culminating in the distance with the statue. Imaginative use has been made of every trick in garden design, to give the impression that the garden is larger, the water deeper, the masonry ancient.

Below left In a raised bed on one side of the steps between the two garden levels, and near the bottom of the stairs that lead down from the decking balcony, tulips 'White Triumphator' and 'Bleu Aimable' flower in spring. A little later there will be the white blossom of the Japanese tree lilac (*Syringa reticulata*).

Right The view of the garden from the house gives an impression of calm, depth and unity. An ancient statue gazes into the pool, which has been tapered towards the far end to give a sense of distance. The raised beds around the edges are planted with Japanese tree lilacs, while on either side of the statue pots hold standard wisterias.

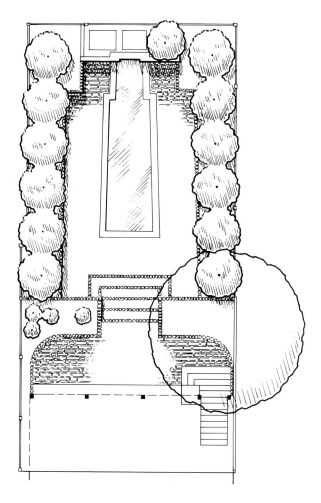

At the end of the garden nearest the house, the deck's arches are reflected in the water of the pool. To give the effect of an expanse of green, the grass is left to grow long, and the steps that link the two levels of the garden have their treads grassed. The 'snow' scattered on the grass and over the surface of the pool has fallen from a flowering crab apple (*Malus floribunda*) near the house.

When the sloping site had been terraced to create clearly defined upper and lower levels, the two levels were linked by shallow steps, with the treads grassed to give an impression of continuous green lawn. Soil from the pool excavation was used to build up the western end of the lower garden, making a flat area 9m/30ft square, and to create raised beds around the edges. To give an illusion of distance, the 7m/24ft pool is tapered towards the far end, and the edges are then stepped in. The pool is only 1.5m/4ft deep – its depth is restricted by a sewer under the garden – but because it has a black lining, and a band of black tiles beneath the pale limestone coping, it appears deeper.

The pool equipment is concealed backstage, behind what appears to be a stone wall and a limestone arch (shown on page 48). In reality they are made of skilfully painted wood. The arch frames and highlights the statue that is the focal point of the garden: an early French bronze, barely 1.2m/4ft high, on a 25cm/10in. pedestal; the arch itself is only 1.5m/5ft, and the pediment above is in proportion, rising to just 2.5m/8ft.

The colour scheme of the planting sustains the cool and peaceful atmosphere. Predominantly white-flowered trees and shrubs are enhanced by grey and blue-grey foliage, with more muted, misty tones towards the back of the garden, to reinforce the effect of distance, and a few pink accents nearer the house.

Below (*left and right*) Raised beds of *Tulipa* 'Pink Impression', edged with dwarf box (*Buxus sempervirens* 'Suffruticosa'), arranged symmetrically on either side of the entrance drive, frame the elegant nineteenth-century house. The crab apples, provide an element of height that is important in the wide space.

A Garden Rich in Colour

It is rare to find a central city garden large enough and so well planted as to have a country air, and Lady Barbirolli feels fortunate to own and tend the third-of-an-acre plot attached to her London flat. Originally designed by Mary Stein, the garden is almost rectangular in shape, with parallel sides, one longer than the other; internal divisions create hidden areas, and boundaries are disguised by abundant and careful planting.

Next to the house is a spacious terrace which supports a raised bed for alpines and large decorative pots planted with shrubs such as pieris and *Rhododendron yakushimanum*. It juts out on one side into a lawn which is surrounded by wide curving borders and separated from the rest of the garden by a line of trellis and shrubs. A shady corner is enlivened by a statue.

Down one side of the garden a wide path is softened by shrubs, bulbs and perennials that arch and spill over it, among them *Nandina domestica*, *Hebe hulkeana*, *Pittosporum* 'Silver Queen', lavatera and *Malva moschata*. The view along the path is partly veiled by a panel of trellis. This is set further back than the main dividing section, showing that the plot extends beyond the barrier, and inviting exploration.

As you round the main divide, a tiny circular rose garden is revealed. It is set in the corner of a second lawn, which also contains a tall *Metasequoia glyptostroboides* and a *Cornus controversa* 'Variegata'. The path then turns sharply round its dividing trellis to the far corner, where a rustic seat overlooks a small *potager*.

The rest of the back of the garden is a natural woodland area, with a raised bed full of woodland plants such as snowdrops, hellebores and ferns, and a semi-wild yellow garden, where forsythia and summer-flowering *Jasminum humile* are underplanted with *Lamiastrum galeobdolon*, *Lysimachia repens* 'Aurea' and daffodils. A narrow, shady path leads past a tall *Viburnum tinus*, an amelanchier, a *Taxus baccata* and the fast-growing bamboo *Arundinaria murielae*, back to the terrace.

The whole garden is heavily planted. Climbers such as the shell-pink clematis 'Hagley Hybrid' and the blue 'Perle d'Azur' thread their way through shrubs and up trees and trellis. Roses too are plentiful: in the main border are the hybrid musk 'Buff Beauty', the climbing 'Magenta' and shrubs of 'Schneelicht' and *R. pimpinellifolia*. Up pillars grow 'Aloha' and 'Schoolgirl', and over the dividing trellis 'Gloire de Dijon' and 'Queen Elizabeth' vie with a japonica and a fatsia, to mask the view.

Far left A statue of Don Quixote by the sculptor Gerald Konstom is the focal point of the secluded area nearest the house. The knight appears to be riding out of the woodland area and diagonally across the lawn towards the house. This asymmetrical positioning helps distract the eye from the garden's almost rectangular shape – as, also, do the gentle curves of the surrounding beds.

Left Planted to give height and poise to the garden, *Cornus controversa* 'Variegata', with its wedding-cake tiers, provides a soft background to the small circular rose garden, which is centred round an old sundial. The roses are all in shades of pink and red, and include 'Papa Meilland', 'Mrs Sam McGredy', 'Mischief' and 'Piccadilly'.

Above Soft clumps of plants such as *Alchemilla mollis*, *Helianthemum* 'Wisley Pink' and *Geranium sanguineum striatum* spill over the main garden path during the summer. Brighter accents of colour are provided by the Ligtu alstroemerias and the pillar rose 'Aloha'. The paving leads the eye down to a trellis panel, through which there are tantalizing glimpses of the rest of the garden.

A PENTHOUSE GARDEN

The garden of the New York penthouse owned by art historian Gwen Burgee and her architect husband John was designed by the Burgees with the help of consultant Tim Duval. It is a garden that shows a sure sense of style, combined with a knowledge and love of plants.

The garden is on two levels, and on each there is an imaginative use of restricted space, incorporating areas that are hidden from the city and others that embrace it as a background. The rooftop terrace on the sixteenth floor provides on one side an open sunny space for perennial plants and on the other an area that is reminiscent of a Moorish garden. On the fifteenth floor a heavily planted long narrow terrace emerges naturally from the living room, so that one moves almost imperceptibly from living area to garden.

The rooftop garden is divided into areas that are dramatically different in atmosphere, yet complement each other. On one side white-painted planters surround a sunny area covered with white pebbles, creating a continuous three-sided border with the city skyline as its backdrop. Filling the planters and spilling over the edges are perennials including *Iris*

Left From the cool, dappled shade of the rooftop arbour, the focal point is the formal lily pool with its sparkling fountain. However, the pale slabs of marble also draw the eye down the garden to the far sunny end, where soft mounds of perennials, spilling over the edges of the raised border, add a touch of informality.

Right On the rooftop terrace architectural effects are as important as the planting. A cross-vaulted arch of white latticework, a feature that is light and airy but still has substance, frames the view of the elegantly furnished sunny deck. The planting too has style, in keeping with the formality of the pool and its marble surround. The two raised borders are perfectly matched, each planted with *Artemisia* 'Silver Mound', the floribunda rose 'Europeana' and, standing sentinel, the honey locust *Gleditsia triacanthos* 'Sunburst'.

PETER C. JONES

122

Above Over the balustrade on the west side of the lower terrace is a spectacular view beyond Central Park to the towers of the San Remo apartments. Here the green of the distant trees and the framing foliage on the terrace is set off by the bright accent of the pink pelargoniums.

Right A lattice-screened dining area, to the east of the rooms on the lower floor, provides a gentle transition between apartment and terrace.

sibirica, gypsophila, astilbes, delphiniums, balloon flowers (*Platycodon*), asters, dianthus and sedums. From here the visitor crosses a tiled terrace to a magical area with a gleaming white vaulted arbour and formal pool and fountain. On either side of the rectangular pool is a path of cool marble, and a border with matched plantings of honey locust trees, floribunda roses and artemisia. Woodland ferns grow in the dappled shade of the arched white lattice arbour. Beyond lies a sunny seating area with a surface of wooden decking. It holds elegant white-painted ironwork furniture, and is surrounded by white trellis that is a frame for climbing roses and morning glory.

On the lower terrace, which is tiled, large containers planted with trees and shrubs help to break up the rather corridor-like shape. A dining area shaded by a yellow awning (shown on page 63) leads out from the french windows of the living room. Here, evergreens form a constant green surround, while oleanders bring bright colour. To one side is a narrow, shady 'woodland path' created by two long rectangular planters filled with white birches. This emerges into a sunny sitting area surrounded by low plants of *Juniperus procumbens* 'Nana' and some taller shrubs, including *Rhododendron yakushimanum*, pieris, wisteria and roses. On the other side of the seating area the main 'feature' is a magnificent vista over Central Park. The view is complemented by plantings of evergreen thuja, quince and *Malus* 'Red Jade' for blossom and fruit, and pelargoniums and the hybrid tea rose 'Peace' for flower colour.

THE PLANTS

Gardens in towns and cities are usually small. They tend to be shaded, and they often suffer both from a lack of privacy and from the effects of atmospheric pollution. The plants that follow have been chosen with these constraints in mind: trees and shrubs for the garden's framework; hedges and climbing plants for screening; and perennials, annuals and bulbs that look good in beds and borders or growing in pots.

TREES AND SHRUBS

ABELIA × GRANDIFLORA

There are few shrubs that bloom towards the end of the summer, a time of year when the garden generally suffers from a dearth of flowers. This delightful plant will fill the gap and extend the season's interest. It has unusually bright evergreen foliage with small oval leaves 2.5–6cm/1–2½in. long and half as wide, fringed with tiny teeth. The funnel-shaped flowers, which are palest pink and slightly scented, hang gracefully on slender, arching stems.

This abelia is generally hardy, and even if cut back by frost it will usually put up new shoots the following spring. If you live in a region where the winters are snowbound and punishingly cold, grow this shrub in a sheltered corner against the house wall and cover it for the winter. In ideal conditions, planted in a sunny position in open, loamy

Acer palmatum 'Dissectum Atropurpureum'

soil, it grows to 1.8m/6ft. The prostrate form, 'Prostrata', and the dwarf 'Sherwoodii' grow to only half the height and make decorative container plants. They should all be pruned lightly after flowering to keep them in shape.
EVERGREEN SHRUBS, FLOWERING IN LATE SUMMER AND EARLY AUTUMN
SUN   ZONES 6-9

ACER PALMATUM

The species Japanese maple is a small upright tree, but many of its clones are bun-shaped and low-branching, so they are often classified as shrubs. They have been culti-vated for centuries in Japan, where they are a favourite subject of watercolour artists, highly prized for their cascading form and autumn colour. They were introduced to the West in the early nineteenth century and rapidly gained popularity; many of the best-known arboreta in Europe owe their vivid autumn colours to this species. They make perfect subjects for the town garden, because they grow slowly and take many years to reach their maximum height of about 2.5m/8ft.

The seed of *Acer palmatum* germinates freely and one plant can give rise to a multitude of differing forms. As many good varieties have been selected for hardiness, colour or leaf shape, it is best to obtain a named form from a reliable source. One of the most popular is 'Dissectum Atropurpureum', which has bronzy-crimson leaves all summer. I also like 'Aureum', which has light yellow leaves with fine red margins in spring, turning light green in summer and bright yellow in autumn. There are variegated clones, such as 'Butterfly', which has light green foliage flecked with cream. There are also some forms with attractively marked bark: the coral-red twigs of 'Sango-kaku' (occasionally still sold as 'Senkaki') are a delight in winter, and the foliage progresses from bright green in spring through brilliant yellow in summer to pink tones in autumn. All these varieties like a neutral to acid, moist but well-drained soil; only the strongest

tolerate alkaline conditions. They colour best in a sunny position, except for the variegated clones, which prefer light shade, having a tendency to scorch in strong sunlight.
DECIDUOUS TREES AND SHRUBS, WITH FOLIAGE COLOUR
SUN OR HALF SHADE   ZONES 5-9

BUDDLEJA

My favourite buddleja is the spring-flowering *Buddleja alternifolia*, commonly called the fountain buddleja because of its gracefully weeping habit. The fragrant purple flowers are borne in clusters all the way along the pendulous branches, and long, slender leaves add to the weeping effect. It grows to 3m/10ft or more but can be kept in bounds by careful pruning immediately after flowering; in pruning, take care not to remove the current season's new growth, since it is these shoots that will flower the following year. This buddleja can also be trained as a standard.

The common butterfly bush, *B. davidii*, is so hardy and easy to cultivate that it has become something of a weed, rooting in walls and colonizing neglected gardens. Even so, it is well worth growing one of the good named cultivars: the deep violet 'Black Knight', violet 'Empire Blue' and soft lavender-pink 'Charming Summer' are attractive. These should all be cut back hard in early spring to encourage the new growth which will bear flowers in summer.
DECIDUOUS SHRUBS, SPRING FLOWERING
SUN OR SHADE   ZONES 5-9

BUXUS SEMPERVIRENS

A native of the Mediterranean, western Europe and central America, box has been grown in gardens for centuries. It is not surprising that early gardeners were so quick to recognize its many merits, for it is a most useful plant. Equally happy in sun or light shade, box thrives on any soil, from heavy clay to light sand, and will add a note of decorative elegance to any garden. It can be clipped neatly into all sorts of shapes, which will stay crisp, because the plant grows so slowly. In the seventeenth and eighteenth centuries, geometric shapes, grown in the ground or in pots, punctuated many a garden.

The leaves of the box are small, rounded and leathery, and a beautiful glossy dark green; the flowers, which appear in late spring, are small and insignificant, discernible only by their yellow anthers, but they have a pleasingly sharp fragrance that is released when you brush past a bush.

Box is most frequently found in gardens in the dwarf form, *Buxus sempervirens* 'Suffruticosa', planted as an edging to knots and parterres. With a little patience, gardeners can easily shape box plants into balls, pyramids or cones – or, more adventurously, spirals or peacocks. Alternatively, it is possible to buy box already trained into a variety of shapes.
EVERGREEN SHRUBS
SUN OR SHADE   ZONES 7-9

CAMELLIA

These slightly tender acid-loving evergreens are prized for their glorious blooms, which come in shades of white, pink, peach, orange and red, and sometimes in tones of two colours. Site them where the morning sun will not reach them until any frost has gone. In colder climates they can be grown in pots, so they can be moved into a frost-free greenhouse or conservatory for the winter.

Camellia sasanqua is the earliest to flower, beginning in late autumn and lasting through the winter. This plant will survive temperatures as low as −10°C/14°F, provided that it is sheltered from the wind, and will grow up to 4m/13ft. The species has clear white flowers and there are numerous, mostly Japanese-bred, cultivars with single or double pink, red or white flowers. *Camellia reticulata*, with flowers in shades from pale pink to crimson, comes into bloom in early spring. This shrub usually reaches about 3m/10ft. Next to flower, in mid to late spring, are *C. japonica* and *C. saluenensis* (both available in a range of colours) and the cross between these two species, *C. × williamsii*. This fine hybrid is vigorous, hardy (to −15°C/5°F) and free-flowering: among its many good cultivars are 'J.C.Williams', 'Donation' and 'St Ewe', all with flowers in delicate shades of pink. In

addition to its other virtues, 'Donation' is also one of the few camellias that will let go of its spent blooms, rather than hanging on to them after they have turned a disfiguring brown.
EVERGREEN SHRUBS, FLOWERING IN WINTER
AND SPRING
PARTIAL SHADE   ZONES 8-9

CERCIS SILIQUASTRUM

Legend has it that Judas hanged himself from this tree; hence its common name, the Judas tree. It was introduced to Europe from the Middle East by the Crusaders some six hundred years ago. They were, no doubt, enchanted by the sight of it in spring when it is studded with bright pink flowers. The rounded leaves, blue-green in spring and

In this shady entrance to a light, sunny garden (featured on pages 76–9), gently rounded mounds of slow-growing *Buxus sempervirens* line the borders of an informal curving path, and provide a dark green backdrop for a small statue. The path edges are further softened with an underplanting of ivy and *Saxifraga stolonifera*.

Camellia × williamsii 'Donation'

summer, turn yellow in the autumn, and the flowers are followed by purple seed pods. In a warm, sunny site with well-drained soil the Judas tree grows to 3m/10ft high and a little less wide. The eastern redbud, *C. canadensis*, is a North American native more suitable for cold areas, where it is just as beautiful. Redbud flowers are sometimes used in salads.

DECIDUOUS TREES, SPRING FLOWERING
FULL SUN   ZONES 6-9

CHAENOMELES SPECIOSA

The japonica was introduced from China to Kew by Sir Joseph Banks in 1796, but it was not until some forty years later that Siebold discovered the many spectacular variations and crosses that had been cultivated in Japan for centuries. The cultivars now available to gardeners range from 'Simonii', with bright red flowers, through pink-flowered 'Moerloosei' to snow-white 'Nivalis'. Their fruits resemble miniature golden apples, sometimes flushed red and speckled with grey dots. They make fragrant quince-like jelly and cheese.

Trained against a wall, chaenomeles will eventually make a span of 1.8m/6ft. As a free-standing shrub it will grow to 3.6m/12ft in height and spread, but it takes fifty years to reach this size. It will grow in most soils, but in acid conditions appreciates additional lime at planting time. Pruning is simple: just cut out wispy new growth in summer.

DECIDUOUS SHRUBS, SPRING FLOWERING,
WITH AUTUMN FRUIT
SUN   ZONES 5-9

CHIMONANTHUS PRAECOX

When *Chimonanthus praecox* was introduced to Britain from China in 1766 it was called the 'early Carolina allspice', because it

Cercis siliquastrum

resembles, and is related to, the North American allspice, *Calycanthus*. Its Latin name (derived from the Greek) literally means 'winter flower'. Nowadays it is commonly, and appropriately, called winter sweet: it is one of winter's most deliciously fragrant shrubs. I first encountered it walking to college one brisk, sunny winter morning. It was the gentle scent I noticed first, well before I saw the shrub, with its pale yellow blossoms. On examination these flowers reveal a most intriguing inner cluster of small purple sepals surrounded by a fringe of more showy waxy yellow ones. This is a shrub for the patient gardener, since its flowers do not appear until the plant is five or six years old. The leaves are a plain dark green, turning yellow-green in autumn.

Plant chimonanthus against a warm wall in rich, well-drained soil, choosing a spot close to the house so that you can enjoy the blooms and fragrance whenever you go out of doors. For added interest, try combining it with a summer-flowering climber, such as a large-flowered clematis or *Tropaeolum peregrinum*.
DECIDUOUS SHRUBS, WINTER FLOWERING
SUN   ZONES 6-9

CHOISYA TERNATA
The Mexican orange is a beautifully rounded shrub with dense, shiny foliage that shimmers in the breeze and changes texture with the light. Each leaf is composed of three oval leaflets, which are discreetly aromatic when crushed. The sweetly scented white flowers resemble the flowers of citrus trees – hence the common name. The first flush of blossom appears in spring, and if the shrub is pruned immediately after flowering it can be encouraged to flower again in early summer, and yet again in late summer or early autumn.

Choisya grows to about 2.5m/8ft and is sufficiently bold to associate well with formal architectural elements in the garden, yet free enough to look comfortable in an informal area. I have seen it planted at the front of a shrub border with a mahonia and a white-flowered camellia, and a large-flowered clematis that twined its way through all three shrubs. It also looks good behind smaller herbaceous plants such as *Dicentra spectabilis* and *Geranium endressii*.

Although a native of Mexico, this shrub has proved reasonably hardy in temperate climates; in a cold garden it is best grown in a pot and overwintered in a conservatory or near a window in a cool room.
EVERGREEN SHRUBS, SPRING FLOWERING
LIGHT SHADE   ZONES 7-9

CORNUS ALBA
This hardy shrub has striking shiny red bark that stands out boldly against the snow in winter. It also contrasts well with the yellow bark of *C. stolonifera* 'Flaviramea': the two together, underplanted with snowdrops and winter aconites, are a fine sight. In summer, the dark green oval leaves of *C. alba* make a good background to brightly coloured herbaceous plants. The white (often blue-tinged) berries form after a hot summer and complement the turning leaves in autumn.

In moist soil and left unpruned, *C. alba* will form a thicket of stems up to 3m/10ft in height, spreading by means of underground rhizomes. To contain the rapid growth, the rhizomes should be cut from the main plant with a sharp spade and dug out. Cut the stems back hard in spring to stimulate young bright growth for the following year.

There are three cultivars to look out for: 'Sibirica' has the brightest stems; 'Spaethii' has golden-variegated leaves; and the grey-green leaves of 'Elegantissima' have an irregular creamy white margin.
DECIDUOUS SHRUBS, WITH COLOURED
WINTER BARK
SUN OR SHADE   ZONES 2-8

CORNUS MAS
The Cornelian cherry is a discreet yet very rewarding plant. The pale yellow flowers appear in earliest spring. The foliage is a plain green in summer, but turns reddish-purple in autumn, often hiding the small cherry-like fruits; these are edible (delicious preserved in syrup), but ripen only after a hot summer. Although the Cornelian cherry will grow quite large, it can be restricted by pruning, and I have seen it clipped into a dense arbour. It is most effective in association with a dark evergreen shrub such as *Chamaecyparis lawsoniana* 'Ellwoodii'.
DECIDUOUS TREES, SPRING FLOWERING,
WITH AUTUMN FRUIT
SUN OR SHADE   ZONES 4-8

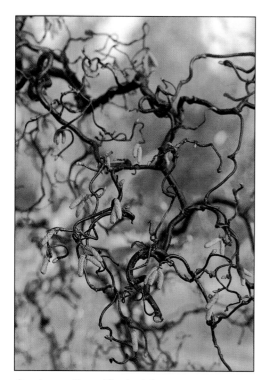

Corylus avellana 'Contorta'

CORYLUS AVELLANA 'Contorta'

The great plantsman E. A. Bowles chose the corkscrew hazel as the first occupant of his 'lunatic asylum', that part of his north London garden reserved for plants with odd mutations. As he remarked in *My Garden in Spring*, the first book of his fascinating trilogy on the garden year, 'It is a most remarkable form, for it never produces a bit of straight wood. The stem between each leaf is curved as though one side had grown much faster than the other and alternating lengths generally curve in opposite directions; frequently they are twisted spirally as well, so that the whole bush is a collection of various curves and spirals.' The leaves too are twisted, which is rather disconcerting, since they look as if they might be suffering from a viral disease such as leaf curl. You may like to draw a veil over them, by clothing the hazel with one of the summer-flowering clematis, such as the white 'Duchess of Edinburgh' or lavender 'Mrs Cholmondeley'. In winter the leafless contorted branches are a fascinating sight. They look stunning against the snow, or against a plain white or against a plain white or pastel-coloured wall. In the spring the tree is covered in clusters of long yellow catkins.

This accommodating plant will grow in almost any position and any type of soil. It is slow-growing, and eventually reaches about 3m/10ft in height.

DECIDUOUS TREES, WITH TWISTED STEMS
SUN OR SHADE   ZONES 3-8

CRATAEGUS LAEVIGATA

Hawthorns make a bright splash of colour in spring, when the dense crown is covered in clusters of five-petalled flowers with fine stamens. In the autumn the glossy red fruits provide additional interest, and, if the birds don't steal them first, they persist well into the winter. This hardy, fast-growing tree reaches about 4.5m/15ft at maturity, when it has gracefully spreading branches; it is resistant to leaf-spot, rust and city pollution. Two cultivars are particularly attractive: 'Crimson Cloud' has red blooms with a white star-shaped area in the centre, and 'Paul's Scarlet' has deep pink double flowers. For particularly cold situations the Canadian cross 'Toba', with white flowers ageing pink, is recommended.

DECIDUOUS TREES, SPRING FLOWERING,
WITH AUTUMN FRUIT
SUN OR SHADE   ZONES 4-7

FATSIA JAPONICA

Fatsia japonica is sometimes confused with the castor oil plant, *Ricinus communis*. Both have large palmate leaves, but they are from different families and have quite different requirements. Fatsia is well known as a house plant capable of putting up with the lowest intensities of light and the driest of conditions. This same tolerance makes it an ideal plant for those difficult shady dry positions in the garden; fatsia will brighten up the darkest corner with its shiny green, nine-fingered, leathery leaves, marked with pale veins. The leaves grow up to 35cm/15in. across and 25cm/10in. long, and are resistant to the worst winds. *Fatsia japonica* 'Variegata' is a good variegated fatsia, with white margins to the leaves, but it is a grafted form, so expensive to propagate and difficult to find.

Some fatsia plants will flower in autumn, producing large flat umbels made up of tiny white blossoms; in mild areas these will develop over the winter into clusters of shiny black berries.

Given the space fatsia can grow to 2.5m/8ft tall, but commonly it stops at about 1.2m/4ft. To keep the plant looking handsome, be sure to pull out dead leaves. Good partners for fatsia include variegated ivy, periwinkle and pachysandra; a clematis such as 'Ville de Lyon' will provide summer adornment.

EVERGREEN SHRUBS
SHADE   ZONES 8-10

FORSYTHIA SUSPENSA

This forsythia grows in the most unruly manner, rambling in every direction and forming a mass of intertwining branches that droop to the ground. But I find such disorder a small price to pay for a plant that revels in a shady position, putting out an abundance of the flowers whose shape and colour have earned it the common name of golden bell. Grown against a wall with support, or against a tree, this plant will reach 9m/30ft or so, but if you grow it as a free-standing shrub you can keep it to 3m/10ft. The golden-yellow flowers appear in early spring, before the leaves emerge, in clusters of six all the way along the pendulous branches. As they grow on the previous year's wood, pruning should be carried out immediately after flowering, so the new wood has time to grow and mature before the next spring. I like to grow forsythia with white daffodils and brunnera underneath, followed by hostas and crane's bill geraniums, and then the tall deep blue monkshood. A large-flowered purple clematis adds interest later in the year.

The forsythia most suited to growing as a hedge is the hybrid *Forsythia × intermedia* 'Spectabilis', or its sport 'Lynwood'; both have *F. suspensa* in their parentage.

DECIDUOUS SHRUBS, SPRING FLOWERING
SHADE OR SUN   ZONES 5-9

HAMAMELIS MOLLIS

The true witch-hazel is the autumn-flowering *Hamamelis virginiana*, a native of the eastern United States which was introduced to Europe in 1736. The Chinese species, *H. mollis*, was not introduced till 1888, but it is much more striking, and more useful, as the flowers appear in mid-winter, long before the leaves, and can well withstand sub-zero temperatures. This shrub grows to a maximum height of about 1.8m/6ft, the angular, upward-turning branches forming a distinctive vase-like silhouette. The leaves are heart-shaped and turn rich coppery-yellow in the autumn. The fragrant, many-petalled, spidery flowers are borne in clusters all along the previous year's stems. In the species they are deep golden-yellow; they are much paler in my favourite variety, *H. mollis* 'Pallida'.

The species has also been crossed with *H. japonica*, giving rise to a number of good cultivars under the general name of *H. × intermedia*. Among the best are those bred at Kalmthout Arboretum in northern Belgium, including the bicoloured (red and ochre-yellow) 'Jelena', the coppery-red 'Diane' (named after the wife and daughter of the arboretum's owner); and, from the United States, 'Arnold Promise', a primrose-yellow selection raised at the Arnold Arboretum.

DECIDUOUS SHRUBS, WINTER FLOWERING, WITH AUTUMN FOLIAGE COLOUR
HALF SHADE   ZONES 5-8

HYDRANGEA MACROPHYLLA

Mophead hydrangeas, or hortensias, are very useful summer plants, flowering late in the season when, often, there is little else in bloom in the garden. Miss Jekyll used them a lot, to plug gaps in the summer border, and in pots around courtyards, especially to emphasize entrances.

The attraction of *Hydrangea macrophylla* lies in its fresh green serrated and deeply veined leaves and its enormous globular flower heads, entirely made up of sterile florets. In open ground it will grow to 2.5m/8ft, but it can be contained by pruning.

These hydrangeas are not very hardy, and in colder climates they are best grown in pots, so that they can easily be moved under cover for the winter. The flower heads should be left through the winter, for protection; in spring, the branches can be cut back to a pair of fat leaf buds, and will soon begin to put out fresh green growth. Alternatively, hydrangeas can be grown anew each year from cuttings taken in late summer; the cuttings can be rooted in a shaded cold frame but must be taken into a frost-free greenhouse or conservatory before the winter begins. Neither

Hamamelis mollis 'Pallida'

new cuttings nor established plants need much water until about the middle of spring, and then they drink a great deal and require regular feeding. In alkaline or neutral soil the blue cultivars need to be dosed with alum or aluminium sulphate to keep their colour.

I particularly recommend the following cultivars: 'Ami Pasquier', deep pink with a dwarf habit; 'Madame Emile Mouillère', an old white cultivar and still one of the best; and the dwarf 'Souvenir de Président Doumer', dark blue in acid soil or when treated with aluminium, otherwise dark red.

DECIDUOUS SHRUBS, FLOWERING IN LATE SUMMER AND AUTUMN
LIGHT SHADE   ZONES 8-9

JUNIPERUS SCOPULORUM 'Sky Rocket'

This narrow, elegant juniper, a native of North America where it is known as the pencil cedar, is particularly useful in a small garden, as it gives accent and height but takes up very little space. After ten to twelve years it will measure up to 4.5m/15ft and still have a girth of only 30cm/12in. A pair makes

a good frame for a gateway. For added interest, try using *Juniperus scopulorum* as a support for the flame nasturtium, *Tropaeolum speciosum*: the bright green leaves and scarlet flowers of this hardy climber create a spectacular effect threading through the dark blue-grey foliage of the tree. Virtually any well-drained soil suits this juniper.

EVERGREEN CONIFERS
FULL SUN   ZONES 4-9

KERRIA JAPONICA

This shrub was named in honour of William Kerr, a gardener at The Royal Botanic Gardens at Kew, who, in 1804, found the double-flowered form growing in China. It was not until 1834 that the more attractive single form was introduced.

Kerria japonica is a tough, upright shrub with suckering stems that, in all but the coldest areas, remain green throughout the winter. The single form grows to about 2m/7ft, the rather more vigorous double form, 'Pleniflora', to 3m/10ft. The flowers of the single kerria are five-petalled and rose-like; those of 'Pleniflora' rather resemble pompons. In both forms they are golden-yellow, and appear in abundance in late spring and then sparsely and sporadically throughout the summer. As the first flush of flowers fades, the nettle-like, toothed and oval leaves appear, their fresh green making a good background for summer-flowering plants.

Kerrias are equally happy in sun or shade and are not demanding as to soil; pruning consists of little more than the occasional removal of old stems after flowering. Grow a large-flowered clematis such as deep purple *Clematis* 'Jackmanii Superba' or lavender-blue 'Mrs Cholmondeley' through its branches, for added summer interest.

DECIDUOUS SHRUBS, SPRING FLOWERING

SUN OR SHADE   ZONES 5-7

LABURNUM × WATERERI 'Vossii'

The Germans commonly, and very appropriately, call the laburnum 'golden rain' (*Goldregen*) because of the appearance of its vivid yellow racemes of pea-shaped flowers. As a small tree, up to 4.5m/15ft, it is useful in town gardens and it is easy to grow, thriving in all but the most waterlogged of soils. The supple branches can be trained into an arch, or, if space allows, a tunnel. An underplanting of a purple allium will add to the stunning effect.

The cultivar 'Vossii' was selected from a cross between *L. alpinum* and *L. anagyroides* and was raised in Holland late in the nineteenth century. It produces abundant flowering racemes up to 60cm/24in. long, but very few of the poisonous green seeds which children easily mistake for edible peas. If you want a real conversation-stopper, try the grafted cross + *Laburnocytisus adamii*, which bears not only purplish-yellow flowers but also the distinct yellow and pink flowers of its parents *Cytisus purpureus* and *Laburnum anagyroides*, with much the same habit as the latter. It is difficult to come by, but fun if you can acquire it.

DECIDUOUS TREES, FLOWERING IN EARLY SUMMER

SUN OR SHADE   ZONES 5-7

LAURUS NOBILIS

Where it has space the bay laurel can grow to 6m/20ft, making a small, dense tree (often multi-stemmed, because if it is cut back by a severe frost it responds by putting out new growth). In a smaller garden it can easily be kept to 1.2m/4ft or less and trimmed to form a standard, pyramid or cone that will act as a focal point; a pair of bay trees in pots can be used to frame an entrance. The secret of growing a bay tree successfully is to plant it in good loam, protect it from wind, and give it lots of water and top-up feeds during the growing season.

The bay laurel has a long and distinguished history: in antiquity, wreaths woven from the branches of this noble plant were used to crown emperors – and victors in the Olympic games. The aromatic leaves, one of the traditional components of a *bouquet garni*, are oval, dark green and slightly leathery. If you clip your bay regularly you will both keep the plant in good shape and have plenty of leaves to use in cooking; use secateurs to cut out individual leaves, or branches that have grown too long; hedge clippers can damage the leaves, scarring them and making them susceptible to disease.

EVERGREEN SHRUBS

LIGHT SHADE   ZONES 7-10

LONICERA FRAGRANTISSIMA

Lonicera fragrantissima can grow to 2.5m/8ft and will flower for several weeks, even in a sunless position; it must, though, have warmth in the summer if the tender new growth is to ripen sufficiently to enable it to withstand the coldest winters. In mild areas the plant behaves almost like an evergreen, keeping most of its leaves. The leaves themselves, however, have little else to commend them, and it is a good idea to plant a large-flowered clematis alongside to liven up the shrub during the summer.

When winter honeysuckle is grown as an individual shrub, it is best to keep it in shape by cutting back old branches to the ground after flowering; it can also be grown as a hedge, and then it should be pruned more lightly in spring.

DECIDUOUS SHRUBS, WINTER FLOWERING

SUN OR SHADE   ZONES 6-9

MAGNOLIA STELLATA

This magnolia is deservedly popular for its sweetly scented white flowers, produced freely even when the tree is only a few years old. It is a compact tree, growing slowly to an ultimate height that rarely exceeds 3m/10ft, though its width may be rather greater, and its tolerance of pollution makes it an ideal plant for an urban garden.

Unlike many magnolias this species is tolerant of lime, though in an alkaline soil it does benefit from the addition of copious amounts of peat at planting time. The distinctive furry grey winter buds open in spring, before the leaves appear, into the star-shaped flowers, with twelve or more narrow petals. A few buds may suffer damage from late frosts, but the tree flowers so abundantly that this scarcely matters. For a charming spring picture, try underplanting it with blue *Muscari armeniacum*.

DECIDUOUS TREES, SPRING FLOWERING

SUN OR SHADE   ZONES 5-9

MAHONIA JAPONICA

The mahonias are sturdily reliable shrubs, hardy in all but the coldest areas, and thriving in any well-drained soil. Moreover, they are happy growing in the shade of buildings or trees, which makes them invaluable plants for the town garden. *Mahonia japonica*, my favourite, is a slow-growing, erect evergreen shrub which will reach a height of over 1.8m/6ft. The pinnate leaves, composed of numerous glossy dark green spiny leaflets, are 30–45cm/12–18in. long; the new leaves, when they emerge in spring, are a delicate rose-red. The flowers are pale yellow and richly scented, appearing any time from late autumn, but usually towards the end of winter, in clusters emerging from the tips of the previous year's growth.

There are other mahonias that are well worth considering. *M. aquifolium*, the Oregon grape, has golden flowers and looks spectacular when the bunches of black fruit mature in late summer. Of the hybrid mahonias the most commonly available is *M. × media* 'Charity'. This is much like *Mahonia japonica*, but faster-growing – not always an advantage in a small garden.

EVERGREEN SHRUBS, WINTER FLOWERING

SHADE   ZONES 5-8

Nandina domestica

MYRTUS COMMUNIS

Following an old tradition (for the plant has long been associated with love), the young Queen Victoria's wedding bouquet contained a sprig of myrtle. A native of the wild, fragrant scrub of the Mediterranean *maquis*, myrtle was first grown as a garden shrub in the sixteenth century. It was much favoured in Britain during the seventeenth century, when clipped evergreens were at the height of their popularity.

Myrtle is a delightful plant to have near the door or under a window, as the broad, glossy leaves are aromatic, and the delicate, scented white flowers that bloom in late summer are a delightful bonus when the season is drawing to an end. In the open ground myrtle can grow to 3m/10ft; in a pot it will reach about 1.2m/4ft. Pruning is entirely at your own discretion. I like to clip mine in spring to keep it trim; it is easily cut into simple architectural shapes to grace the garden.

EVERGREEN SHRUBS, FLOWERING IN LATE SUMMER
SUN   ZONES 8-10

NANDINA DOMESTICA

This remarkable shrub is quite commonly grown in the southern United States. It is ubiquitous in Japan, from where it was introduced to the West in the nineteenth century. There it is often planted close to the house (hence the species name, *domestica*), where it spreads to form groves, believed to be inhabited by benign spirits: *Nandina* derives from the Japanese *nanten*, meaning heavenly or sacred bamboo.

I have never understood why it is not better known in Europe. Perhaps the fact that it is not bone-hardy has proved a deterrent, but though it needs protection from cold winds, it will grow happily in a sheltered town garden. I am pleased to see that it is now offered by some nurseries.

Although related to berberis, *Nandina domestica* has long, bamboo-like stems. In spring the young growth is bright coppery-pink; this turns green as it ages and is tinged with purple in the autumn. In warm climates it bears trusses of white flowers, followed by translucent red berries. The species grows to 1.5m/5ft or more, but there is a dwarf form, 'Nana Purpurea', which is only 45–60cm/18–

MALUS

The ornamental crab apple trees deserve to be used much more widely. Personally, I prefer them to the flowering cherries (*Prunus*), the other large genus of small spring-flowering trees. *Malus* cultivars are available in a range of spring colours: 'Liset' is a pleasing deep red, and there are many clear pinks, often fading to white, as in 'Snow Cloud'; an added bonus is the scent of many forms. The foliage colour is equally varied: the leaves of some cultivars, such as the American *Malus* 'Strawberry Parfait' have early red tints turning green; *M.* 'Brandy-wine' has purple or coppery leaves turning russet-orange in the autumn. The fruits range from bright red in 'Red Sentinel' to golden-yellow in 'Golden Hornet'. Most make delicious jelly. The trees are usually vase-shaped, sometimes pendulous, reaching approximately 6m/20ft. Wallflowers planted underneath will flower before the trees blossom.

DECIDUOUS TREES, SPRING FLOWERING, WITH AUTUMN FRUIT
SUN OR SHADE   ZONES 4-8

MESPILUS GERMANICA

If you really want to bring a feeling of past times to your garden, try planting a medlar. This attractive small tree has been cultivated since the Middle Ages, originally for the sake of its brown fruit, which is best left on the tree to go over-ripe before being eaten. The woody texture is not to everybody's liking, but it makes good jelly with a delicate taste, described by some as akin to that of the guava. The tree has a rounded habit, rather flattened at the top, and rarely exceeds 6m/20ft in height. The leaves are quite large, up to 12cm/5in., oval in shape and nearly stalkless; they turn golden-yellow in the autumn. The solitary flowers are white, sometimes tinged with pink.

Two other ancient fruit trees, the black mulberry, *Morus nigra*, and the red-flowered quince, *Cydonia japonica*, are similar in habit to the medlar, and equally hardy.

DECIDUOUS TREES, FLOWERING IN EARLY SUMMER, WITH AUTUMN FRUIT
SUN OR SHADE   ZONES 6-8

24in. and turns bright scarlet in the autumn. Both are happiest in fertile, freely draining acidic loam. A small acer or a *Fatsia japonica* would be a good companion – the acer providing complementary autumn colour, the fatsia contrasting leaf shape.

EVERGREEN SHRUBS, WITH FOLIAGE COLOUR
SUN OR PARTIAL SHADE   ZONES 6-9

PHILADELPHUS

The charm of the philadelphus lies in its spectacular early summer display of scented white flowers. The true mock orange, *Philadelphus coronarius*, from south-east Europe, is known to have been in cultivation as long ago as the sixteenth century, and *P. inodorus*, from the south-eastern United States, has been grown since the mid-eighteenth century. Many more species and a range of hybrids have been introduced and bred since the nineteenth century.

'Belle Etoile' is a good philadelphus for a small garden. It only reaches 1.5–1.8m/5–6ft in height, and it is quite hardy. There are smaller cultivars, such as 'Manteau d'Hermine' and 'Etoile Rose', which grow to about 90cm/36in., but most of them need a warm, sheltered position, as they do not withstand hard winters. 'Virginal' and 'Minnesota Snowflake' are hardy, but grow larger, reaching 2.5m/8ft. To contain their vigour, I would advise pruning the oldest stems down to the ground on a three-year cycle. The blossoms appear on second-year wood, so cutting all the branches back would result in a mass of uninspiring green leaves the next year. To extend the season of interest, try growing *Clematis macropetala* or a blue summer-flowering clematis through the philadelphus.

DECIDUOUS SHRUBS, FLOWERING IN EARLY SUMMER
SUN   ZONES 5-8

PIERIS JAPONICA

Introduced to the West from Japan in 1870, this beautiful spring shrub is often planted alongside rhododendrons, because both like moist, acid soils.

The chief enemies of pieris are cold winds and early frosts that desiccate the tender young growth. Given adequate protection, and an annual late winter mulch of peat or leafmould, it will form a compact, bushy shrub, eventually reaching 3m/10ft, clothed to the ground with beautiful foliage. The young leaves emerge in spring in shades of pink, and later turn a glossy dark green. The foliage of the cultivar 'Bert Chandler' is especially striking: it starts salmon-pink, and turns cream and then white before becoming green. The flower buds are formed in the autumn but do not open until spring. The flowers then last for several weeks; their colour varies from pure white ('Purity'), through shell pink ('Blush') to deep pink ('Daisen'). Many gardeners consider that the seed pods detract from the handsome shape of the shrub. If you cut off the flowers as they fade, you will ensure not only stronger foliage growth but also a better flower display the following year.

EVERGREEN SHRUBS, SPRING FLOWERING, WITH SPRING FOLIAGE COLOUR
SUN   ZONES 5-9

PRUNUS LAUROCERASUS 'Otto Luyken'

This is a hardy hybrid cultivar, raised in Germany where the continental winters can be bitterly cold. Its ability, unusual in a broad-leaved evergreen, to withstand long periods of sub-zero temperatures makes it extremely useful, and since its introduction in the late 1960s it has been used extensively in landscaping projects, though it is less common in gardens. It was developed from the large, and only marginally hardy, cherry laurel. A dwarf form, barely reaching 1.2m/4ft, it has a horizontal, compact shape. The slender, pointed leaves are of a consistent dark green, and the flowers are fragrant, freely borne in 5–12cm/2–5in. long racemes in late spring, and followed in hot summers by purplish-black fruit. In addition to all its other virtues, this shrub is not at all particular as to soil or position.

EVERGREEN SHRUBS, FLOWERING IN LATE SPRING
SUN OR SHADE   ZONES 6-9

PRUNUS × SUBHIRTELLA 'Autumnalis'

This tree never fails to arouse interest and surprise, for it bears its heaviest crop of flowers in the depths of winter. The white flowers may be small but they are numerous, and they continue to open for several months, from late autumn to early spring. When fully grown this graceful tree stands about 7.5m/25ft high and has a tendency to weep slightly. The narrow leaves take on rich autumn colour late in the season. Small sprigs can be cut and brought indoors to open during the coldest weather. The sight of one of these trees, viewed from the kitchen window of my London flat, was enough to brighten even the dullest winter day. When I recently moved to a house with a large country garden, I was delighted to find one blooming there too. The pale pink cultivar, 'Autumnalis Rosea', is equally charming.

DECIDUOUS TREES, WINTER FLOWERING
SUN OR LIGHT SHADE   ZONES 5-8

PYRACANTHA COCCINEA

The firethorns are handsome evergreen shrubs, related to cotoneaster but distinguished by their vicious thorns, and the serrated edges to their leaves. *Pyracantha coccinea* is highly adaptable. When it was first introduced to cultivation in the eighteenth century it was trained as a standard; it can also be grown as a free-standing bush or trained against a wall, and a row of them will make a dense hedge. A pyracantha can reach 5m/16ft against a wall, but in the open, without support, it takes many years to grow beyond 1.8m/6ft.

The branches of the firethorn are a mass of small creamy-white flowers in late spring. By the autumn these have turned to equally numerous bright orange berries that will remain on the shrub as long as the birds permit. It is from the flame colour of the berries that the plant takes its common name. The cultivars differ principally in the colour of their fruits. 'Lalandei' has orange-red berries, and you can find pure red berries in some of the hybrids, including 'Watereri' and 'Fiery Cascade', while *Pyracantha rogersiana* 'Flava' has bright yellow berries. All these varieties will grow in any fertile soil, and they are tolerant of pollution and most exposures. They can be pruned immediately after flowering: just shorten any over-long growths.

EVERGREEN SHRUBS, FLOWERING IN LATE SPRING, WITH AUTUMN FRUIT
SUN OR SHADE   ZONES 6-9

PYRUS SALICIFOLIA 'Pendula'

The weeping pear was discovered in the Caucasus by the German botanist and explorer P. S. Pallas, in the late eighteenth century. It is a striking tree that is seen to best advantage if it is planted as a solitary specimen in a lawn or courtyard, or in a pair flanking a gateway. The long, flowing skirt of pendulous branches is clothed in downy, narrow, willow-like leaves that are silvery early in the season, turning to grey-green later in the summer. The flowers are creamy white and are followed by small pear-shaped fruit in the autumn. (Unfortunately, the fruit is not good for eating or cooking.) The weeping effect can be heightened by training the leader up a pole to 4.5m/15ft or so; the branches will then form a cascade, trailing all the way to the ground.

DECIDUOUS TREES, WITH SILVER FOLIAGE
SUN OR LIGHT SHADE   ZONES 5-8

RHODODENDRON HYBRIDS

In recent years American breeders have been introducing many first-class rhododendrons, taking over from the British and Dutch, who traditionally led the field. One of the finest new American dwarf cultivars is the white 'Dora Amateis', and another American innovation is the very hardy 'P.J. Mezitt', a shrub that will bloom even if there is frost about, and cheers the dullest days with its lavender-pink flowers and bronze foliage. Neither grows to much more than 1.2m/4ft. Rhododendrons, of course, do best in rich acid soil: humus can be added to the soil in the form of peat or, better still, leafmould, applied regularly as a deep mulch. Mulching also has the benefits of conserving the moisture that rhododendrons need in summer, and providing nutrients. The shallow roots of the rhododendron resent disturbance, so don't dig the mulch into the soil – leave it to the worms to work it in. You should also avoid hoeing between the plants. Deadheading encourages abundant flowering the following year, and the spent flowers can conveniently be added to the mulch under the plant. Remove the dead flowers at the point where they join the stem of the plant, taking great care not to cut the new bud beneath.

EVERGREEN SHRUBS, SPRING FLOWERING
LIGHT SHADE   ZONES 5-8

Philadelphus 'Belle Etoile', with *Clematis* 'Prince Charles'

RHODODENDRON LUTEUM

Rhododendron luteum, which used to be *Azalea pontica*, comes from the Caucasus but grows well in cooler climates. The species name *luteum* refers to the yellow flowers that come in varying shades – from very pale to quite deep egg yolk – and are shaped rather like those of the honeysuckle. They have a delicate fragrance that I always associate with May visits on warm afternoons to the Royal Horticultural Society's garden at Wisley in Surrey, where this shrub has been naturalized in the woodland surrounding the car park. *Rhododendron luteum* can grow to about 2.5m/8ft in good conditions, and has a twiggy, slightly whimsical habit: it can, though, be pruned after flowering to remove unwanted growth and keep the shape compact. The leaves that follow the flowers turn red and orange in autumn, bringing a touch of fire to the garden.

DECIDUOUS SHRUBS, SPRING FLOWERING, WITH
AUTUMN FOLIAGE COLOUR
LIGHT SHADE   ZONES 5-9

ROBINIA PSEUDOACACIA 'Frisia'

One of the loveliest of garden trees, this golden-leaved form of the false acacia was introduced from Holland as recently as 1935. However, the species is a native of eastern and central America, found from the Appalachians southwards, which has been in cultivation since the early eighteenth century.

The false acacia is best planted in soil that is only moderately fertile. It grows quite fast when young – it can reach a height of 4.5m/15ft in ten years – and if conditions are too favourable, growth can be so rapid that the wood becomes brittle and whole branches snap off in the wind.

'Frisia' bears racemes of fragrant white flowers in early summer, and throughout the summer has a light crown of yellow-green pinnate leaves, which turn butter-yellow in the autumn. Its upright habit allows bulbs and other shade-tolerant plants to thrive underneath. A purple-leaved berberis such as *Berberis thunbergii atropurpurea* or *B. thunbergii* 'Rose Glow', or a purple smoke bush such as *Cotinus coggygria* 'Notcutt's Variety' or 'Royal Purple', makes an admirable companion. Another good foil is the dark purple tulip 'Queen of Night', which flowers in early summer. A slightly more tender but equally attractive alternative to this robinia is the golden-leaved form of the honey locust, *Gleditsia triacanthos* 'Sunburst'.

DECIDUOUS TREES, FLOWERING IN EARLY SUMMER, WITH FOLIAGE COLOUR
SUN OR LIGHT SHADE   ZONES 5-8

The golden-leaved *Robinia pseudoacacia* 'Frisia' keeps its intense colour from spring to autumn. Here, its brightness is set off by the dark leaves behind, and the purple foliage of *Berberis thunbergii atropurpurea* to one side. Lysimachia and sedums thrive in the shade beneath.

SHRUB ROSES

There are so many good shrub roses that it is difficult to make a choice. Each one seems worth a place, for its flower colour, scent, habit, foliage tints or historical associations. But most town gardens are small, and space is at a premium, so the wise gardener looks for those varieties that give maximum value in terms of compactness and length of display. The following are just a few recommendations for roses that either flower repeatedly through the summer, or, in addition to their flowers, have good autumn leaf colour or spectacular hips.

'Reine Victoria' has the typical round, many-petalled flowers of the Bourbon group to which it belongs. The pink blooms are fragrant and long-lasting and hold their heads up against the gentle grey-green foliage.

'Souvenir de la Malmaison', named after the Empress Josephine's famous rose garden near Paris, was introduced in 1843. The flowers, which are flushed with the palest pink when they open, fade to white. They have a delicious scent and are repeat blooming.

'Reine des Violettes' is a vigorous plant that makes a good background shrub against a sunny wall. It has the virtue of being almost thornless. It blooms repeatedly throughout the summer, and the near-purple flowers turn cerise-red in overcast conditions.

Rosa sericea pteracantha is a species rose with large translucent red thorns that are brilliant in winter sun. The leaves are delicate and ferny and the single white flowers are followed by dark red hips.

Shrub roses do not require anything like the amount of attention necessary for the successful flowering of hybrid teas or floribundas. You need do no more than cut out annually any old stems, to keep the bush in shape and give new shoots space to develop. The best flowers appear on the side shoots of the previous year's vigorous stems, so these are the ones to encourage. Roses that are perpetual flowering or bear showy hips should be pruned in late winter or early spring; once-flowering roses can be pruned immediately after flowering.

DECIDUOUS SHRUBS, SUMMER FLOWERING
SUN OR LIGHT SHADE   ZONES 4-10

SENECIO 'Sunshine'

Senecio 'Sunshine' is valuable for its attractive evergreen foliage: the grey-green leaves are fringed with a crisp margin of white, and the undersides are a much paler green, soft and felt-like. Planted in a well-drained, sunny position, this senecio will also bear masses of daisy-like yellow flowers that are attractive to bees and butterflies and often continue from the beginning of summer to early winter.

When fully grown this shrub makes a rounded mound, about 1m/3ft 4in. tall and as wide. It needs some pruning to keep it in shape. It is often planted in a grey/blue/pink colour scheme, for the harmonizing effect of its leaves; in this case it should be pruned in spring, before the flowers appear. If, however, you want it to bloom freely in a yellow/orange colour scheme, prune after the flowers have faded, taking out unwanted growth.

'Sunshine' is a tough plant that withstands atmospheric pollution well, so it is suitable for a front garden exposed to traffic fumes. The branches are somewhat brittle and will occasionally snap in a strong wind; do not worry if this happens, for the plant will quickly recover.

EVERGREEN SHRUBS, SUMMER FLOWERING
SUN   ZONES 8-10

SORBUS

Rowan, or mountain ash, and whitebeam both belong to the genus *Sorbus*, a most valuable family of small trees (up to about 4.5m/15ft) with attractive qualities in all four seasons. The whitebeams (*Sorbus aria*), which are often planted as street trees, form upright specimens with dense crowns of oval leaves: these shimmer in the breeze as the wind alternately reveals the grey-green upper surface and the downy silver underside. Clusters of white flowers appear in late spring and are followed by showy red berries that can remain on the tree throughout the winter – though birds find them attractive, and will strip a tree in days if a harsh winter denies them alternative sources of food. The mountain ash (*S. aucuparia*) is distinguished by its pinnate leaves with sharply toothed leaflets. The flowers and berries are similar to those of the whitebeam, but in some species, such as *S. cashmiriana*, the fruit is ivory white and therefore less attractive to

the birds. All species are highly tolerant of urban pollution and grow well in most soils.

DECIDUOUS TREES, SPRING FLOWERING, WITH INTERESTING FOLIAGE AND WINTER BERRIES
SUN OR SHADE   ZONES 3-7

VIBURNUM × BODNANTENSE 'Dawn'

First raised at Bodnant, the Welsh garden of Lord Aberconway, in 1935, this is one of the finest winter-flowering viburnums. It is a narrow upright shrub, growing to 1.8m/6ft in height. The flowers, which are freely borne in late winter and are frost-resistant, are deep pink in bud, opening to white flushed with pink, and have a heady, sweet fragrance: the scent has been described as like a mixture of nutmeg and honey. The foliage is deep green, turning purple in the autumn.

This viburnum likes a well-balanced and freely draining loamy soil, and in cold areas is best planted in a protected position.

DECIDUOUS SHRUBS, FLOWERING IN LATE WINTER
SUN OR LIGHT SHADE   ZONES 6-8

VIBURNUM DAVIDII

This attractive evergreen viburnum, introduced to the West from China in 1904, is a useful plant that makes ideal ground cover in a shady garden. Though *Viburnum davidii* scarcely ever grows to more than 60cm/24in. high, a mature shrub will form a rounded, compact dome that spreads to around 90cm/36in. across. The handsome leaves are a thick, shiny dark green, with paler green undersides, and narrowly oval with pointed ends, shallow teeth and three conspicuous nerves, or ribs, running along their length. The grey-white flowers appear in early summer and are followed in late summer by metallic greeny-blue fruits that rise in striking clusters above the foliage, and subsist long into the winter. For successful pollination you will need a mixture of male and female plants, so it is worth buying plants of known sex from a reliable nursery.

This viburnum succeeds best in a fertile, well-drained, neutral to alkaline soil and needs some protection from the worst cold.

EVERGREEN SHRUBS, FLOWERING IN EARLY SUMMER, WITH AUTUMN FRUIT
SHADE   ZONES 7-9

HEDGES

BERBERIS

The berberis, or barberry, family includes many named varieties and hybrids, most of which make good, hardy hedges, resistant to city pollution. The yellow or yellow-tinted flowers provide a splendid spring display, attracting bees and other insects, and are followed by red or blue egg-shaped fruit in autumn.

Because it is so spiny, a berberis hedge is a powerful deterrent to the incursions of neighbouring cats and dogs. However, this benefit has to be weighed against the disadvantage that pruning is a painful process. Wearing stout gardening gloves is a help, but you must take care to clear up all the pruning debris, or else risk being speared by the winter-hardened thorns while you are innocently weeding the following spring.

Several varieties are available from nurseries. *Berberis thunbergii* is a compact plant with outstanding autumn foliage colour and red berries. Its form *atropurpurea*, which is perhaps the hardiest of the barberries, has purple autumn foliage.

The evergreen species are less hardy but, I think, more beautiful. *Berberis × stenophylla* is a cross which arose in the 1860s between *B. darwinii* and *B. empetrifolia*. It has gracefully arching stems which reach 1.8m/6ft and drip with orange-yellow scented flowers in spring, and grey-blue berries in autumn. Many named selections have been developed from this hybrid, including 'Gracilis', which never grows to more than 1.2m/4ft in height, so is useful for smaller gardens.

Barberries are very resilient and will thrive in any reasonably well-drained soil. To create a berberis hedge, place the individual plants at 75cm/30in. intervals. You can trim unwanted growth immediately after flowering, but leave some flowers to form autumn fruit.

EVERGREEN SHRUBS, SPRING FLOWERING
SUN OR SHADE   ZONES 6-9

Ilex × altaclerensis 'Belgica Aurea'

CARPINUS BETULUS

The numerous twiggy branches of the hornbeam are easy to clip, which makes this tree an ideal subject for hedging and topiary; for centuries gardeners have been trimming and training it to make hedges, arbours, tunnels and palisades. The hornbeam's leaves resemble those of the beech, but they are smaller and toothed. Their autumn colour is slightly more golden than the copper of beech leaves, but they lose their colour and drop sooner. The seventeenth-century diarist John Evelyn wrote in his *Discourse of Forest Trees* that 'The Places it chiefly desires to grow are in cold hills, stiff ground, and in the barren and most exposed parts of woods.' It is, indeed, altogether a hardier tree than the beech, more tolerant of clay and the extremes of acid or alkaline soil, more sturdy against the wind and perfectly happy growing in shade.

Hornbeam will make a hedge up to 2.5m/8ft high. Plant seedlings 30cm/12in. apart. Leave them untrimmed for the first two

years, to establish strong leaders; thereafter, until the hedge is well established, just trim to shape in mid-summer. Once you have a dense hedge you can clip in late summer or early autumn to remove unwanted growth and restrict it to the desired height.

DECIDUOUS TREES
SUN OR SHADE   ZONES 5-9

FAGUS SYLVATICA

Beech is not only one of the finest of forest trees, it is also invaluable in the garden, for making hedges with architectural form and strength. Like the hornbeam, beech breaks into many branches when it is cut, to create a dense, leafy barrier. It is a joy in late spring, when the soft, delicate, almost translucent young green leaves begin to unfold. The leaves turn a rich copper-brown in the autumn and remain on the hedge through the winter until the early spring.

Beech will grow on most soils provided that they are freely draining; it does not like

saturated soils so will not thrive in a hollow that collects water, or on the heaviest clays. It will make a hedge of up to about 2.5m/8ft high. Seedlings should be planted 35cm/15in. apart, at any time from mid-autumn to early spring; each needs to develop a strong leader, but you can cut back any long lateral shoots in mid-summer. Once the hedge is established it can be trimmed at any time from late autumn to early spring.
DECIDUOUS TREES
SUN OR SHADE   ZONES 5-9

ILEX

Ilex aquifolium, also known as the English holly, is slow-growing but makes a dense dark green hedge, up to about 2.5m/8ft high and tolerant of pollution. It has characteristically prickly leaves and small white flowers that hide at the base of the leaves in early summer.

The plants can be male, female or bisexual. Bisexual hollies produce red berries freely in the autumn, and these will persist (birds willing) long into the winter. The male forms do not produce fruit, and you can only count on berries from females if they are planted near males, to ensure pollination. It is worth investing in named varieties from a reliable source, so that you can be certain of the sex. If you then plant a mixture of male and female forms you should get a good crop of berries. I particularly like *Ilex aquifolium* 'Silver Queen', which is male (in spite of its name) and has green and silver variegated leaves, and 'Handsworth New Silver', a female with similar variegation. *Ilex aquifolium* 'Golden Milkboy' (male) and *I.* × *altaclerensis* 'Belgica Aurea' (female) are good gold-variegated hollies. Among the bisexual cultivars, I would recommend *I. heterophylla* 'Pyramidalis', which is freely fruiting and has fewer spines to the leaf – a great asset when pruning.

Sadly, the evergreen hollies are not completely hardy in severe continental climates, but some deciduous species and cultivars that have been bred in America specifically to withstand these conditions are now widely available. These include *I. verticillata* 'Winter Red' and the *Ilex* × *meserveae* group of blue hollies: 'Blue Princess'

Osmanthus delavayi

and 'Blue Stallion', planted together, produce a magnificent display of berries.

Hollies don't like being moved, so you will need to take care when transplanting them: seedlings should be planted out either in early autumn, when growth is just ceasing, or late spring, when it is about to start again, and as much soil as possible should be taken with the roots, to avoid any damage. To make a hedge they should be spaced at 90cm/36in. intervals. Trim holly hedges in late summer or early autumn.
EVERGREEN AND DECIDUOUS SHRUBS, WITH WINTER BERRIES
SUN OR HALF SHADE   ZONES 4-9

LIGUSTRUM OVALIFOLIUM 'Aureum'

Privet is a plant that grows swiftly and does well in hostile city air, and for these reasons it was once extremely popular as a hedging plant, especially for suburban front gardens. People are now inclined to be rather dismissive about it. It is true that the leaves tend to become dusty, and in cold winters they will drop off, revealing an untidy skeleton. The species will also rapidly lose its shape if it is not pruned frequently. However, the golden form is slightly slower-growing,

and the leaves are a jolly, sunny gold that makes an admirable backdrop to a yellow and blue garden. It grows to about 1.2m/4ft and is best clipped twice a year, first in late spring, once it has recovered from any winter damage, and again in late summer, to keep it neat and tidy. Look out for any branches that have reverted to the plain green form and cut these out immediately, as they grow more vigorously than the golden ones and will quickly take over if not removed. Seedlings can be planted at 60cm/24in. intervals to make a hedge. Alternatively, you might consider planting some bushes singly, as privet also makes a good subject for clipping into a topiary cone or pyramid, or for cultivating as a standard.
SEMI-EVERGREEN SHRUBS
SUN OR SHADE   ZONES 5-9

OSMANTHUS DELAVAYI

Osmanthus delavayi is one of my favourite evergreens, and I strongly recommend it for planting either as a hedge or as an individual shrub in any town garden that is sufficiently warm and sheltered. In colder regions it is well worth growing in a pot that can be brought into the conservatory in the winter.

The osmanthus was introduced by the

Abbé Delavay, one of those courageous
French missionaries who brought us so many
of our best garden plants, from seed collected
in China in 1890. It has small, leathery oval
leaves, fringed with a rim of minute teeth.
The sweetly fragrant flowers are creamy
white in colour, shaped like tiny trumpets,
and grow in bunches all the way down the
stems. I like to cut long stems before the
flowers are fully open, to bring indoors where
the heat hurries them on and accentuates the
scent. The shrub is slow-growing, but in
sheltered conditions and well-drained soil it
will reach anything between 1.8m/6ft and
6m/20ft. To make an osmanthus hedge,
plant a row of shrubs, spacing them
at intervals of 30cm/12in. or so. The
hedge can be trimmed to the desired
height immediately after flowering.
EVERGREEN SHRUBS, SPRING FLOWERING
SUN OR PARTIAL SHADE   ZONES 6-9

POTENTILLA FRUTICOSA
'Goldfinger'

'Goldfinger' is a recent selection of the true
Potentilla fruticosa, or shrubby cinquefoil,
which was first recorded by the English
botanist John Ray as long ago as 1670. This
potentilla makes a low-growing informal
hedge that will flower all summer long: with
its delicate silvery foliage and bright yellow
flowers it looks quite spectacular, and if you
plant it in your front garden you will find that
it is much admired by passers-by.

'Goldfinger' reaches its maximum height of
1.2m/4ft in about three seasons. Thereafter it
continues to put out graceful arching stems,
but it remains compact and well-behaved,
especially if you cut it back quite hard in the
early spring. It spreads well, so if you space
your plants 75cm/30in. apart in well-drained
soil in a sunny position the gaps will quickly
fill, and by the end of the second season you
should have a good solid hedge.
DECIDUOUS SHRUBS, SUMMER FLOWERING
SUN   ZONES 2-8

PRUNUS LAUROCERASUS
PRUNUS LUSITANICA

These two glossy-leaved laurels have been in
cultivation since the seventeenth century and
are often used to create evergreen hedges up
to about 2.5m/8ft high. Neither, however, is
perfectly hardy and both like well-drained
soil in a reasonably warm spot sheltered from
the wind.

The Portugal laurel, *Prunus lusitanica*, is
perhaps marginally the more hardy. It has
slenderly oval shiny dark green leaves; the
stalks and young stems are variously tinted
dark red. On an unpruned specimen long
racemes of white flowers will appear in early
summer, and these are sometimes followed
by dark purple fruit. The cherry laurel,
P. laurocerasus, has much larger oval leaves
that are a paler green and somewhat leathery
in texture. The rather insignificant flowers
appear in spring.

Both laurels can be planted in autumn or
spring, and to make a hedge the young plants
should be about 60cm/24in. apart. You can
prune these laurels in late spring or early
summer, using secateurs to cut out unwanted
growth: don't use shears or a hedge trimmer,
as these will only damage the leaves and
detract from the appearance of the hedge.
EVERGREEN SHRUBS
SUN   ZONES 7-9

RHODODENDRON
YAKUSHIMANUM hybrids

In recent years the number of small hybrid
rhododendrons available to the public has
increased considerably – a great boon for
town gardeners, who have little space to grow
the banks of blowzy rhododendrons that one
associates with the great country gardens.

Most of these small hybrids derive from
one of the tiniest rhododendrons,
Rhododendron yakushimanum. This is a slow-
growing, small, compact shrub: the first plant
that was introduced to Britain in the 1930s
was only 1.5m/5ft high and 2m/7ft across
forty years later. The leaves are dark green
above, downy brown beneath, and about 7cm/
3in. long, but these are all but invisible in
spring when the bushes are covered in great
trusses of yellow, red, pink or white flowers.
In recent trials conducted by the Royal
Horticultural Society the merits of twenty-six
hybrids were assessed, and of these I would
recommend 'Caroline Allbrook' with lavender
blooms, 'Golden Torch', pale yellow, 'Hydon
Dawn', rose-pink, and 'Titian Beauty', red.
The last two have colours that complement
each other well, and would make a fine mixed

Rose 'Fritz Nobis'

hedge of intermingled rose and red. All four
are wide-spreading shrubs and can be
planted at intervals of 60–90cm/24–36in.
They will tolerate a little sun, but do best in
the light shade cast by an overhanging tree.
The species comes from one of the
southernmost islands of Japan, where the
rainfall and humidity are high, and it needs
plenty of moisture. The hybrids, however, do
surprisingly well on quite dry sites.
EVERGREEN SHRUBS, SPRING FLOWERING
LIGHT SHADE   ZONES 4-8

ROSE 'Fritz Nobis'

'Fritz Nobis' is one of those shrub roses
whose spread tends to be greater than their
height, so it is a good subject for planting as a
hedge. It takes up too much space to be
suitable for the smallest gardens, but it is
well worth growing, for the pleasure it gives,
if you have the room. In mid-summer the
bush is covered in clusters of large flowers,
shaped rather like those of a hybrid tea, in
the most beautiful tones of pink, and sweetly
fragrant. The stems arch gracefully to about
1.8m/6ft, and are covered in clear green
leaves. The thorns are rather large, so

Taxus baccata, the common or English yew, grows to make handsome dark green hedges that will define the garden's structure, and provide a satisfyingly solid background for garden furniture and flowers.

the autumn and contrasting well with the vivid scarlet of the hips.

The most spectacular hybrid is perhaps 'Fru Dagmar Hastrup', which bears recurrent clusters of clear pink single flowers with cream stamens, followed by deep red hips. I also like 'Blanc Double de Coubert', a double form, and the single 'Alba', both with pure white flowers. 'Alba' produces hips freely; sadly, 'Blanc Double de Coubert' is rather less generous. Finally, I am particularly partial to the dark crimson cultivar 'Roseraie de l'Haÿ', as much for its beauty and fragrance as for the memories it evokes of my visits to the *roseraie*, or rose garden, of the same name, planted at the end of the last century just south of Paris.

Like most shrub roses, *Rosa rugosa* requires little pruning: weak and old stems can be cut out in late winter to keep the hedge in shape, and from time to time it may be necessary to remove any branches that are outgrowing their allotted space.

DECIDUOUS SHRUBS, SUMMER FLOWERING
SUN OR LIGHT SHADE   ZONES 3-8

TAXUS BACCATA

Taxus baccata, the common or English yew, is considered by many to be the most noble of all the species suitable for hedge-making. Certainly, a yew hedge is invaluable as a wind barrier, as a screen against an unsightly view, as a foil to the bright colours of summer blooms, and as a handsome green presence in the garden throughout the winter.

Yew is often described as a slow-growing plant but, given adequate protection, in less than ten years it will grow to 2.5m/8ft – more than anyone would wish for in a small garden. It is also most amenable to being cut back hard, clothing itself anew with myriads of green shoots within a season. Clipping encourages the yew to produce a dense mat of dark green, needle-like leaves which make a splendid backdrop to an annual or perennial

remember to wear a pair of gloves when you prune this rose. Grown as a hedge, however, 'Fritz Nobis' does not need much pruning – I simply cut out weak and old growth in late winter.

Other roses suitable for making a hedge are 'The Fairy', 'Felicia' and 'Coupe d'Hébé', all with pink flowers, cerise-pink 'China Doll', yellowy-cream 'Penelope' and white *R. pimpinellifolia*. Generally, if you plant roses 1m/3 ft 4in. apart they should make a good, dense hedge in two seasons.

DECIDUOUS SHRUBS, SUMMER FLOWERING
SUN OR LIGHT SHADE   ZONES 4-8

ROSA RUGOSA

Rosa rugosa is a shrub rose that is resistant to most diseases and grows quickly to make a compact, dense and prickly intruder-proof hedge. The single forms not only have deliciously fragrant blooms but also bear succulent large fat hips; these remain on the plant well into the winter and can be used in flower arrangements or made into a clear, nutritious jelly. The stout stems are a browny grey and covered in a multitude of thorns. They grow little longer than 1.5m/5ft – often less, in my experience. The leaves are a lush pale green, colouring more or less yellow in border. Both the foliage and the berries of the yew are poisonous, but this need not be a concern in a town garden, where there are no livestock to graze on the leaves; berries are rarely produced on a hedge, because clipping removes most of the previous year's growth, on which the flowers, and later the berries, are borne.

As most yews are propagated from seed, hardiness varies markedly from plant to plant, so it is wise to buy seedlings from a well-established specialist nursery which will reject the weaker specimens and supply plants that are two or three years old. The hybrid *T.* × *media*, raised at the turn of the century at the Hunnewell Arboretum in Massachusetts, is hardier than the species. Several clones have been selected from this hybrid, including 'Hicksii', which has larger foliage than *T. baccata*.

Yews can be planted in early autumn or early spring. It is worth preparing the ground well before you plant a yew hedge. For the best results, you should dig a trench 60cm/24in. deep and the same in width, line the bottom of the trench with well-rotted manure, and ensure that the soil you return is well broken up and free-draining. Yews prefer slightly alkaline soil, so it is a good idea to add lime if your soil is acid. Seedlings of 30–90cm/12–36in. should be planted, approximately 60cm/24in. apart. Thereafter it is important to keep the soil beneath free of weeds and grass, which will compete with the young hedge for nitrogen (but be careful not to disturb the tree roots during weeding). It is a good idea to mulch the soil with well-rotted manure once it has warmed up in the spring.

Don't cut the hedge at all during the first year, while it is getting established. Subsequently it can be trimmed to shape, but you should not cut the leader until the hedge has developed to the height you require: just trim the lateral growth in late summer or early autumn. You may have the good fortune to acquire a garden that already has an established yew hedge: if it has become old and overgrown you can rejuvenate it by pruning back hard in early spring.
EVERGREEN TREES
SUN OR LIGHT SHADE   ZONES 6-8

THUJA OCCIDENTALIS
THUJA PLICATA
The *arbor vitae*, or tree of life, *Thuja occidentalis*, is a native of the Great Lakes area of North America and is one of the hardiest of those evergreen conifers that can be clipped satisfactorily into a hedge. The green spring and summer foliage assumes a pleasing brownish hue in the autumn and winter. The western red cedar, *Thuja plicata*, is a native of the west coast of America and is less hardy, but has much darker glossy green foliage, which many people prefer. Both exude a strong smell of orange when the leaves are crushed, and this is a sure way of distinguishing them from certain cypress trees which they resemble. *T. occidentalis* will grow to 18m/60ft in the wild, while *T. plicata* is even larger, growing to 60m/200ft. Fortunately, both can be maintained as hedges at a modest height of 1.5m/5ft. They should be planted 60–90cm/24–36in. apart and clipped regularly in late summer, beginning in the year they are first planted, to achieve a close texture. However, the leader should be allowed to reach its required height before it is clipped.
EVERGREEN TREES
SUN OR LIGHT SHADE   ZONES 3-8

VIBURNUM OPULUS 'Compactum'
This viburnum is an attractive specimen shrub for the small garden, and in a slightly larger garden it can be used to make a stunning informal hedge. Like so many of the viburnums, it has attractions in most seasons of the year. A compact form of the guelder rose, it bears cymes of small white flowers in early summer; the outer flowers are sterile but more showy than the fertile inner ones, which turn into heavy bunches of translucent red berries in the autumn. The berries contrast well with the golden tints of the ageing, maple-like palmate leaves, and subsist well into the winter after the leaves have fallen. The shrub has a dense habit and, planted at 90cm/36in. intervals, will grow to form a 1.5m/5ft hedge that requires little pruning to keep it in shape.

There are many other named selections of the guelder rose which grow a little taller and are laxer in habit: they are less suitable for hedging, but worth considering as accent shrubs in a border. 'Aureum', which has golden foliage throughout the seasons, is particularly striking in the shade, while 'Roseum' is good in the sun. The latter is sometimes sold under the name 'Sterile', and it is also known as the snowball tree. These names are descriptive of the plant's tightly packed blossom balls, which consist only of sterile florets, and so are not followed by the autumn display of berries.
DECIDUOUS SHRUBS, SPRING FLOWERING
SUN OR SHADE   ZONES 3-8

VIBURNUM TINUS
Viburnum tinus, the laurustinus, is a native of the Mediterranean and, sadly, grows well only in mild conditions; however, a town microclimate is often warm enough for it to succeed. It was introduced to Britain in the sixteenth century and was a favourite 'green' – the term used for conspicuously verdant plants – of seventeenth-century gardeners. (Other popular 'greens' were *Phillyrea angustifolia*, *Rhamnus alaternus* and *Myrtus communis*.)

The laurustinus has oval leaves that are dark shiny green above and lighter below. They are evergreen, and a good foil to the small white flowers that are borne in flat cymes 5–10cm/2–4in. across, and bloom continuously from late autumn right through until the late spring. Given sufficient warmth and sunshine, the flowers are followed by dark blue berries that eventually ripen to black. This viburnum will grow in any well-drained soil, and though it does best in sun, it will tolerate shade. There are several cultivars, but the best for hedge-making is 'Eve Price', which rarely exceeds 1.5m/5ft. This cultivar is also distinguished by the pink blush of the flowers in bud.
EVERGREEN SHRUBS, WINTER FLOWERING
SUN OR SHADE   ZONES 7-9

CLIMBING PLANTS

ACTINIDIA KOLOMIKTA

The French call this twining climber *herbe aux chats* and in Britain it is sometimes known as the cat plant, for cats find it irresistibly attractive. If it is not protected they will rub against the foliage and chew young shoots to destruction. The naturally variegated heart-shaped leaves, 7–15cm/3–6in. long, are white at the tips, pink and green towards the downy stalks. Most of the small white flowers lie hidden by the large leaves, but they are sweetly fragrant and are sometimes followed by small, yellow, gooseberry-like edible fruit. Although this actinidia will grow in the shade, spreading to 3.6m/12ft, the colouring develops best in sunshine.

For a larger area of wall, the more vigorous *Actinidia arguta*, sometimes also called the Yang-tao, grows to 20m/65ft or more and has deep green leaves some 10cm/4in. long, with similarly fragrant white flowers. For warmer climates, or a sunny protected spot, there

Actinidia kolomikta

is the Chinese gooseberry, or kiwi fruit, *A. chinensis*, with browner, hairy stalks, yellow flowers and plump, juicy fruit.
DECIDUOUS CLIMBING SHRUBS, WITH FOLIAGE COLOUR
SUN OR SHADE   ZONES 4–10

AKEBIA QUINATA

In the wild this vigorous climber, twining its way up trees, can reach 12m/42ft, but in cultivation it can easily be contained by careful pruning of the strongest shoots. It is valuable for covering pergolas and trellis, and for camouflaging sheds and garages, and will thrive in most situations, provided it is planted in a rich, well-drained loam.

In mild climates this akebia is nearly evergreen, but it is completely deciduous in cold conditions. The attractive leaves are a fresh, translucent green, and are composed of five leaflets arranged around the end of a slender stalk. The racemes of pale flower buds appear in early spring, opening in late spring into fragrant chocolate to maroon flowers. So long as they are not hit by a late frost and the summer is reasonably long and sunny, the flowers will develop into peculiar sausage-shaped fruits that split open when ripe to reveal jet-black seeds embedded in white pulp.

Akebia quinata looks well with *Clematis tangutica*, or a yellow-flowered rose such as 'Golden Showers'.
SEMI-DECIDUOUS CLIMBING SHRUBS, SPRING FLOWERING, WITH AUTUMN FRUIT
SUN OR SHADE   ZONES 4–9

CELASTRUS ORBICULATUS

The oriental bittersweet is related to the spindle tree (*Euonymus*) and bears equally spectacular fruit in the autumn. It is a strong grower that quickly clothes pergolas, unsightly walls, old stumps and large trees, reaching to 12m/42ft given the opportunity. You can limit its growth by reducing excessively long shoots; otherwise all you need do is cut out old wood towards the end

of summer or in early spring, when all the fruit has dropped off.

The leaves are more or less round, with pointed ends and shallowly serrated edges, and turn yellow in the autumn. The small green flowers appear in early summer, and are followed in autumn by pea-sized green fruits which ripen black and split open to expose the bright vermilion seeds against the ochre-yellow inner surfaces. They remain like this through much of the winter. It is worth seeking out the hermaphrodite form, with male and female flowers on the same plant; otherwise, for successful fruiting, you will need to grow a mixture of male and female plants together.

Parthenocissus tricuspidata and *Cotoneaster horizontalis* make good companions for this climber.
DECIDUOUS CLIMBING SHRUBS, WITH AUTUMN FRUIT
SUN   ZONES 5–8

CLEMATIS large-flowered hybrids

There are, essentially, two groups of large-flowered clematis. The first group flowers in early summer and includes the mauve-pink 'Nelly Moser', lavender 'Vyvyan Pennell' and white 'Marie Boisselot'. Plants in this group require only light pruning: just cut each stem back to a strong pair of buds. The second group flowers in mid to late summer and includes the dark purple *Clematis* 'Jackmanii Superba', rosy-purple 'Victoria' and carmine-red 'Ville de Lyon'. They all need severe pruning. Reduce each stem to just above the base of the previous season's growth, about 75cm/30in. from the ground.

All clematis need plenty of moisture, and their roots must be protected from direct sun: the large leaves of plants such as hostas will provide shade, or the soil can be covered with a mulch, or with stones or granite chippings. The flowering stems will grow up as far as they need in order to find light, easily reaching 3.6m/12ft or more. This makes them ideal for growing through shrubs

to complement or extend the flowering season. The gorgeous big flowers look stunning with roses, viburnums, the purple-leaved smoke tree, hebes, fuchsias or low-growing conifers.

DECIDUOUS CLIMBING SHRUBS, SUMMER FLOWERING
SUN OR SHADE, WITH ROOTS IN SHADE
ZONES 3-9

CLEMATIS MACROPETALA

One of the loveliest of the species clematis, *Clematis macropetala* has great gaiety and freshness. The species was introduced to the West in 1910, from northern China. The small nodding double flowers are about 8cm/3in. across, and they are composed of four blue petals and numerous petal-like staminodes which become paler blue towards the central white stamens. This clematis is not an over-vigorous climber, reaching a maximum height of perhaps 4m/13ft. It is easy to care for, being one of the few clematis that only rarely contracts wilt, and it needs very little pruning – just tidy it up, cutting out old wood, after flowering. There are several good cultivars of *Clematis macropetala*, including the pale blue 'Maidwell Hall', deeper blue 'Blue Lagoon' and blue-pink 'Markham's Pink'. These clematis look lovely cascading over walls or out of pots, and they will grow happily through winter or summer-flowering shrubs such as *Chimonanthus praecox* or *Viburnum opulus* 'Roseum', extending their season of interest.

DECIDUOUS CLIMBING SHRUBS, SPRING FLOWERING
SUN OR HALF SHADE, WITH ROOTS IN SHADE
ZONES 4-9

CLEMATIS MONTANA

Few sights are more satisfying than that of a garden shed, or other obtrusive structure, disappearing under the thick mantle of *Clematis montana* when it flowers in early summer. The abundant flowers make a sea of white petals, each studded with golden stamens, which exude a fragrance

Purple *Clematis* 'Victoria' and wine-red 'Madame Julia Correvon', with *Rosa* 'Mutabilis' and *Lavatera* 'Barnsley'

Clematis montana rubens, with
Lonicera periclymenum 'Belgica'

reminiscent of vanilla. The species is believed
to have been introduced from the Himalaya
in 1831 by Lady Amherst, wife of the
Governor-General of India. The pink variety,
C. montana rubens, flowers even more freely,
with larger blooms, and has purple-bronze
young leaves. Both will grow well in either
sun or shade, provided that the roots are kept
moist and protected from direct sun. *Clematis
montana* and its varieties should be lightly
pruned, to contain the growth, immediately
after flowering, so that the plants have the
rest of the summer to put on the new growth
that will bear the following year's blooms.
DECIDUOUS CLIMBING SHRUBS, SPRING
FLOWERING
SUN OR SHADE, WITH ROOTS IN SHADE
ZONES 3-9

CLEMATIS TANGUTICA

An autumn-flowering climber of great beauty,
this species has thick, waxy golden-yellow
sepals resembling orange peel, followed by
silky tasselled seed heads; the seed heads
develop before the last flowers fade, and
persist well into the autumn. Given support,
Clematis tangutica will grow vigorously to
3m/10ft or more, and only requires light
shaping in early spring. There are a few
selected forms that are well worth seeking
out. 'Bill Mackenzie', named by Valerie Finnis
after the Curator of the Chelsea Physic
Garden, is a particularly vigorous plant with
numerous lemon-yellow flowers that open
wide in the sun. 'Burford Variety' has thicker
sepals of a darker yellow. Grow *C. tangutica*
with *Berberis thunbergii atropurpurea* and a
yellow rose such as 'Lawrence Johnston'.

Clematis tangutica is also often listed under
the name *C. orientalis* (the true *C. orientalis* is
similar, but relatively rare in cultivation).
DECIDUOUS CLIMBING SHRUBS, AUTUMN
FLOWERING
SUN OR LIGHT SHADE, WITH ROOTS IN SHADE
ZONES 5-9

COBAEA SCANDENS

Although *Cobaea scandens*, a native of central
America, was listed in *Curtis's Botanical
Magazine* as long ago as 1784, it has been
little grown in Europe and North America.
This is probably because it is tender, and will
only survive as a perennial in mild, frost-free
areas. However, in my opinion it is well worth
the small extra trouble of growing it as an
annual. Seeds sown in a tray on a warm
window sill can be potted up as soon as the
first pair of leaves appears, and planted out in
a sheltered position once the danger of frost
has passed. A plant will reach 4.5m/15ft in
a year, and will quickly fill a blank piece of
wall or clothe an arbour, attaching itself to
its support by a terminal tendril that grows
from the tip of each branch. Its leaves are
10cm/4in. long and attractively veined.

Cobaea scandens has a variety of common
names, including Mexican ivy, monastery or
cathedral bells and cup and saucer plant. The
first is an allusion to its provenance, the rest
refer to the interesting bell-shaped flowers.
These, the cups, open yellowy-green and
gradually turn purple against the green five-
sepalled calyces, the saucers. *Cobaea scandens*
looks wonderful growing through a yellow
rose, such as 'Royal Gold'.
ANNUAL CLIMBING PLANTS, FLOWERING IN
LATE SUMMER
SUN   ZONES 9-10

COTONEASTER HORIZONTALIS

Cotoneaster horizontalis was first raised from
seeds sent to the Paris Museum in around
1870 by the missionary Père David, a botanist
who introduced many good garden plants
from China. A slow-growing, hardy shrub, it
has a distinctively flat habit, hugging either
the ground or the surface of a wall. It rarely
grows taller than 90cm/36in., but will spread
its branches, geometrically arranged in
herringbone fashion, as wide as 2.5m/8ft. The
glossy dark green leaves are small and
pointed, barely 1cm/½in. long, clustered all
along the branches. In early summer the
branches are studded with pink flowers on
short leafy twigs. These flowers are attractive
to bees. Vermilion berries are formed during
the summer, ripen in autumn and subsist into
the winter, long after the leaves have fallen.

Cotoneaster horizontalis will grow in almost
any soil, thriving best in a moist, fertile,
well-balanced compost, but also tolerating the
dry conditions at the base of a wall.
DECIDUOUS CLIMBING SHRUBS, SPRING
FLOWERING, WITH AUTUMN FRUIT
SUN OR SHADE   ZONES 5-9

EUONYMUS FORTUNEI

This evergreen spindle from Japan is very
hardy. In its juvenile state it will climb walls
and trees or nearly any support, and if none
is available it will creep along the ground,
spreading to 6m/20ft or more. The small,
shallowly toothed leaves cluster all along its
short warty stems, and in cold areas it can be
used to clothe a shady wall or as ground
cover. When it reaches the adult stage the
branches tend to grow more upright, the
leaves become larger and more variegated,
and it bears small pale green flowers.

Euonymus is most often seen growing as a
low shrub, up to 90cm/36in. high, but it will
climb to 3m/10ft against a wall. One of the
best varieties is 'Silver Queen', with leaves
up to 6cm/2½in. long with a wide, irregular,
cream-coloured margin. 'Emerald 'n' Gold' is

Hydrangea petiolaris

heat. As with all vigorous climbers, care should be taken to prevent shoots from creeping under roof tiles or smothering window frames, making them difficult to paint and maintain. This can be achieved by cutting out overgrowth at virtually any time of the year. Although ivies will grow in most soils, they prefer alkaline conditions (hence their liking for the mortar in walls), and some limestone grit incorporated in acid soil at planting time will go a long way towards getting the plants established quickly.

Ivy is available in a great variety of forms and leaf shapes, from tiny, crinkly-leaved dwarf cultivars to the tender *H. canariensis* with its large glossy green leaves. For most town situations *H. colchica* 'Dentata Variegata', the variegated Persian or Colchic ivy, is ideal. It is robust and bears slightly lobed leaves up to 8cm/3in. long, usually slightly less; these are light green with random patches of grey-green and a golden-yellow margin. This ivy looks good with the orange-berried *Pyracantha coccinea*.
EVERGREEN CLIMBING SHRUBS, WITH VARIEGATED FOLIAGE
SHADE   ZONES 5–9

HUMULUS LUPULUS 'Aureus'
The common hop can often be found twining its way through wild hedgerows in Europe, making a thick mat of stems and large vine-like leaves. It is a herbaceous perennial, and consequently dies down completely in the winter, but its speed of growth and coverage is prodigious. Quickly growing to 3.6m/12ft or more, it makes an ideal screen for an unsightly fence; alternatively, it can be used in association with other sturdy climbers to clothe a summerhouse or pergola. The golden-variegated form, 'Aureus', is particularly valuable: it will brighten up any shady corner, and associates admirably with purples (you could try it with *Vitis vinifera* 'Purpurea', or *Cobaea scandens*).

The flower heads are hidden behind overlapping bracts, and it is these, the hops, that are harvested for their lupulin, one of the main ingredients in the manufacture of beer. Hops also dry well, and make a good display in winter arrangements.
HERBACEOUS CLIMBING PERENNIALS
SUN OR PARTIAL SHADE   ZONES 6–9

distinctive, erect, dwarf shrub that is ideal for a small garden, reaching little more than 50cm/20in. when grown as a free-standing shrub. It has attractive leaves, up to 4cm/1½in. long, margined with golden-yellow for most of the year but with a pink tint all over the leaf in winter.
EVERGREEN CLIMBING SHRUBS, WITH INTERESTING FOLIAGE
SUN OR PARTIAL SHADE   ZONES 5–9

HEDERA COLCHICA 'Dentata Variegata'
Ivies are the most useful of plants, growing in the shadiest positions, and quickly making a self-clinging screen. In some countries gardeners are advised not to grow ivy against house walls, because the roots can penetrate soft mortar joints, but in Germany they encourage ivy on houses, believing it to be an effective insulator that helps to conserve

HYDRANGEA PETIOLARIS

The climbing hydrangea, called by some *Hydrangea anomala petiolaris*, is a spectacular plant. Ideal for covering a problematic shady wall, it also looks well scrambling up a tree, or grown as a free-standing shrub. It is attractive in all seasons: even when it is bare of leaves in winter the rusty brown bark traces a sinuous pattern on a supporting surface, and the dried blooms resemble a mass of delicate spider's webs. In spring, pointed light green buds emerge and grow into handsome veined, serrated, rich green leaves. The flower heads, consisting of great corymbs of showy white sterile flowers surrounding the smaller, duller white fertile ones, are the triumph of the plant; they appear in early summer and persist to early autumn.

Hydrangea petiolaris is slow to establish and when grown as a wall plant appreciates guidance for the first two or three years; once it has gained a grip on a wall, attaching itself by means of small aerial roots, it will grow much faster, and ascend to 18m/60ft or more if allowed. Pruning may be required, in early spring, to contain its growth, but if you have the space it is best left to grow in its own free way.

DECIDUOUS CLIMBING SHRUBS, SUMMER FLOWERING

SHADE   ZONES 5–8

JASMINUM NUDIFLORUM

The delicate appearance of winter-flowering jasmine is deceiving: it is a tough survivor, a hardy Chinese treasure that will grow in any soil and flower in the shadiest position, and is all the more precious because it flowers at a time when other blooms are scarce. It does, though, need some shelter from desiccating cold winds, which will burn the tips of the branches and stop its growth.

The flowers stud the plant with golden six-petalled stars continuously throughout the winter, starting at the end of autumn in mild areas, later in colder districts. After the flowers have faded the angular green stems are clothed by pairs of small bright green trifoliate leaves.

Winter jasmine does have a rather lax and twiggy habit, and it will sucker all over the garden if allowed, so it needs support and strict management. It enjoys tumbling over

the side of a wall, with the main stem attached to the wall. The branches will grow to 3m/10ft or more but can be controlled by pruning. You can cut the flowering stems back to the main stem each spring, and every few years the stem itself should be cut back to the ground to encourage strong new growth. You can also begin tidying up the plant during the winter, by cutting small sprigs in the bud and bringing them into the house, where the buds will open in a matter of hours. *Mahonia aquifolium* is a good companion plant for winter jasmine.

DECIDUOUS CLIMBING SHRUBS, WINTER FLOWERING

SUN OR SHADE   ZONES 5–10

JASMINUM OFFICINALE

The old-fashioned white summer jasmine, with its heady fragrance and graceful twining habit, has traditionally been considered an appropriate emblem for amiability. It is an accommodating plant, flowering best in poor soil, although a little feeding in its early years will help it to gain height. It looks splendid growing up a trellis, in association with roses, or trained up an old fruit tree.

The jasmine's flowers are its chief glory, and from early summer to late autumn an established plant is covered in heavily scented four or five-petalled white blooms. The leaves, in feathery pairs each composed of five to nine small leaflets, are a delicate green when they first emerge, darkening later. The stems remain green throughout the year, giving a pleasant if tangled effect even during the winter. They do not need annual pruning, but an occasional sorting out helps, as they can grow 1.8m/6ft or more in a season and in mild conditions may ultimately reach 12m/42ft.

DECIDUOUS CLIMBING SHRUBS, SUMMER FLOWERING

SUN OR LIGHT SHADE   ZONES 8–10

LATHYRUS LATIFOLIUS

Sweet peas are among my favourite flowering plants. I grow long rows of annual sweet peas, mainly in blocks of creamy white and pale pink, in my sunny walled garden. I also have the perennial sweet pea, *Lathyrus latifolius*, climbing through trellis on the shady side of the house. This was grown from seeds that I

gathered from a plant in my grandmother's garden in France where, for as long as I can remember, and probably well before that, it has bloomed faithfully every summer, bringing a bright purple splash to the shady yard. I always marvel at the way it shoots up from nothing to a height of 3m/10ft in a single season, before flowering and setting seed and then disappearing completely for the winter.

It has to be said that the perennial sweet pea is not an elegant plant. It has coarse stems and dull grey-green narrow leaves, and the undiscerning tendrils cling to any support, including other stems, so that it ends up in a tangled mess. Even so, the wealth of sweetly scented, lobed flowers makes up for all its shortcomings. There is a white form, 'Albus', that is reputed to be a far finer plant, but it also requires a great deal more sun.

Perennial sweet peas will grow in most reasonably fertile soils. They can be propagated either from seeds or by division of the black roots in spring.

HERBACEOUS CLIMBING PERENNIALS, SUMMER FLOWERING

SUN OR SHADE   ZONES 4–9

LONICERA PERICLYMENUM

'The Woodbinde groweth in woods and hedges, and upon shrubs and bushes, oftentimes winding it selfe so straight and hard about, that it leaveth his print upon those things so wrapped'; so John Gerard described the European native honeysuckle in his *Herball (or Generall Historie of Plantes)* of 1597. He grew this and the 'double Honisukle' in his own London garden.

In cultivation the honeysuckle usually grows to about 3m/10ft and needs support for its twining stems. The leaves vary in shape: some are oval, others somewhat like an oak leaf, and most are green above and slightly blue beneath. The flowers, which blossom from early summer to autumn, are creamy white at first and age golden-yellow. Bunches of translucent red berries develop even while the late blooms are still flowering. The honeysuckles are valued above all for the sweet, heady scent of their flowers. As the degree of fragrance varies considerably from plant to plant, it is worth seeking out one that has been propagated from a parent known to be sweetly scented.

Lonicera periclymenum 'Belgica'

The two cultivars most commonly available are *Lonicera periclymenum* 'Belgica', the early Dutch honeysuckle and *L. periclymenum* 'Serotina', the late Dutch, both of which have pinkish-purple tinges in their flowers. All honeysuckles like their roots to be shaded but flower best in the light; however, the Hungarian hybrid *L. × tellmanniana* will flower well even in the shade. Honeysuckles look their most romantic with pink roses.
DECIDUOUS CLIMBING SHRUBS, SUMMER FLOWERING
SUN OR LIGHT SHADE, WITH ROOTS IN SHADE
ZONES 4–9

PARTHENOCISSUS TRICUSPIDATA

The self-clinging Boston ivy is most useful for clothing a large, shady wall or covering an unsightly building. An extremely vigorous plant, it will reach 18m/60ft within a few years in most conditions; as it is also resistant to pollution it is particularly valuable in shady town gardens.

On young plants the leaves are broadly oval with a heart-shaped base and toothed margins, while on older plants they consist of three distinct leaflets, each on a short stalk. They are light green when they emerge in spring, become a deeper green during the summer, and are at their most spectacular in the autumn, when they turn scarlet and crimson. In warm climates this ivy also bears small dark purple autumn fruits. You can prune Boston ivy as hard or as lightly as you choose, depending on how much you want to contain its growth; but at the minimum you should keep it out of drains and away from roofing tiles, windows and doors.

There are two commonly grown cultivars: 'Lowii' has smaller leaves and the leaves of 'Veitchii' are purple.
DECIDUOUS CLIMBING SHRUBS, WITH AUTUMN FOLIAGE COLOUR
SUN OR SHADE   ZONES 4–9

POLYGONUM AUBERTII
POLYGONUM BALDSCHUANICUM

The Chinese *Polygonum aubertii* and the closely related Russian vine, *P. baldschuanicum*, are two spectacularly vigorous climbers. Either will rapidly take over any garden structure, and many people are justifiably wary of their exuberance. However, they are invaluable to anyone with a deeply shaded site where nothing else will make any impact. Their shared nickname of 'mile a minute' aptly describes the rate at which the young shoots grow in the spring, waving their tips in the wind ready to twine themselves around any available support. It is not always easy to distinguish between the two plants. *Polygonum aubertii* has flowers along its stems, while the flowers of *P. baldschuanicum* are clustered towards the stem tips. But in flower both become a white, frothy mass, which turns pink as the seeds develop. They flower best in the sun, but if planted in shade will climb as high as necessary to find the light.
DECIDUOUS CLIMBING SHRUBS, SUMMER FLOWERING
SUN OR SHADE   ZONES 4–9

ROSA FILIPES 'Kiftsgate'

This rose is another climber that is so vigorous some might regard it as folly to include it in a small urban garden. However, I have often admired one that grows through a lone apple tree in the tiniest of London gardens. It not only looks marvellous from below, it is also a source of delight to both the owners and their neighbours as they look down on it from their upper windows.

The original plant of this clone, growing at Kiftsgate Court in Gloucestershire, is now some 12m/42ft high and still growing. Kiftsgate has the space to allow the rose free rein: in most town gardens it would be wiser to prune unwanted growth in winter. The young leaves of 'Kiftsgate' are coppery-red, turning a solid green with a hint of blue in it as they mature. The abundant small, scented flowers are borne in long panicles, opening creamy and turning to a glistening white. The hips are the size and shape of marbles, and turn from orange to scarlet. Be careful when you are pruning; the spines are ferocious.
DECIDUOUS CLIMBING SHRUBS, SUMMER FLOWERING
SUN OR PARTIAL SHADE   ZONES 6–9

ROSE 'Madame Alfred Carrière'

'Madame Alfred Carrière', with its quantities of fragrant scented flowers, is one of my favourite climbing roses. It is an amenable plant, which will grow happily against a shady wall, reaching 6m/20ft if left to grow unchecked. The growth is predominantly upright and you will need to train some

Rose 'Madame Alfred Carrière'

branches to grow horizontally if you want it to cover a wall, but the stems are fairly lax, which makes training relatively easy. The large, shiny light green leaves are borne on green stems that have the virtue of being nearly thornless, so pruning is a painless task. In any case, this rose needs little pruning – just cut out the longer and older branches in winter. The sweetly scented double flowers appear in great quantity early in the summer and continue for a whole month. They are palest pink in bud, open creamy and fade to white. After the first flush of flowers more will appear spasmodically through the rest of the summer, and there is a second, less profuse burst of blooms in the early autumn. Grow this beauty with the perennial sweet pea (*Lathyrus latifolius*) and *Clematis* 'Nelly Moser', and plant *Alchemilla mollis* around its base.
DECIDUOUS CLIMBING SHRUBS, SUMMER FLOWERING
SUN OR SHADE   ZONES 6–9

ROSE 'New Dawn'
Introduced nearly sixty years ago, this rose has never been surpassed, even though it has been used to breed many successful hybrids.

The virtues of 'New Dawn' would fill a catalogue: it is free-flowering, fragrant, exceptionally hardy, grows happily in shade, and is resistant to most diseases – particularly mildew, which attacks so many other climbing roses. Because its growth is mainly lateral it rarely reaches a height exceeding 6m/20ft, but it will quickly cover a fence or wall, and makes a delightful and welcoming sight climbing over a porch or doorway.

'New Dawn' begins to flower in mid-summer, and will then bloom for the rest of summer and into autumn. The blossoms are dark pink in bud, fading to pale pink as they open, and the petals retain their colour for a time even after they fall, carpeting the ground below. The leaves are a glossy green.

Prune this rose in late autumn, cutting out older branches, to ensure vigorous renewal by young stems the following spring. I like to grow one of the late-flowering, large-flowered clematis hybrids through the framework of the rose: the purple flowers of 'Gipsy Queen' or 'Lady Betty Balfour' provide a perfect complement to the pink of 'New Dawn', and the clematis roots benefit from the shade offered by the rose.
DECIDUOUS CLIMBING SHRUBS, SUMMER FLOWERING
SUN OR LIGHT SHADE   ZONES 6–9

SOLANUM CRISPUM 'Glasnevin'
A native of Chile and Peru, this beautiful climber is not fully hardy in colder conditions; all the same, given a sheltered, sunny spot and well-drained soil, it frequently does well in the microclimate of a town garden. Provided that it has plenty of winter protection, it will survive temperatures as low as −10°C/14°F. Even if the foliage is cut back by frost, it will often push out healthy, vigorous new stems, up to 3.6m/12ft long, the following season. In districts that get really cold weather it can be grown in a container and taken into a conservatory in winter; alternatively, you can take cuttings in late summer, bring them indoors and plant them out the following spring.

Solanum crispum is related to the potato and the tomato, and it has similar purple flowers with contrasting bright yellow anthers which stand out well against the pale green leaves. The flowers are borne in profuse clusters, from mid-summer to late autumn, and are delicately perfumed. The best time to prune unwanted growth is spring, before the start of the growing season. It is advisable to provide some support for the new stems, tying them back to a trellis or to nails embedded in the mortar of a wall.

In a warm area *Cytisus battandieri* makes a good companion for *S. crispum*. Where it is a little colder you could try a yellow rose, such as 'Frühlingsgold'.
EVERGREEN CLIMBING SHRUBS, FLOWERING IN SUMMER AND AUTUMN
SUN   ZONES 8–10

TROPAEOLUM SPECIOSUM
The flame nasturtium is a wonderful plant to grow up the shady side of a dark green conifer, or through the broad leaves of spring-flowering evergreens such as camellias and rhododendrons. The slender stems will grow up to 3.6m/12ft in a season, the delicate pale yellow-green five or six-lobed leaves shine out against darker foliage, and in summer the scarlet flowers are a spectacular sight. Occasionally fruit is produced: this is pale green at first, and later turns dark blue. You can try sowing the ripe fruits, two or three to a pot; transplant the seedlings in spring, as soon as they are large enough to handle, taking care not to disturb the roots. It has to be admitted, however, that the flame nasturtium is not an easy plant to establish, and in some gardens it refuses to grow. The fleshy rhizomes should be planted a good 15cm/6in. deep for protection from the extremes of both cold and heat, mild conditions being essential for success. *Tropaeolum speciosum* also needs good drainage, and dislikes being disturbed.
HERBACEOUS CLIMBING PERENNIALS, SUMMER FLOWERING
SHADE   ZONES 7–9

VITIS COIGNETIAE
The glory vine is grown principally for its brilliant autumn colour. The slightly lobed leaves grow up to 25cm/10in. long and almost as wide, and are dark green for most of the year, turning crimson above and russet below in the autumn. The colours are most vivid if the vine is planted in a warm, sunny position in well-drained soil.

This vine climbs by coiling its tendrils around any supports they encounter, and in its native Japan it winds through forest trees to a height of 27m/90ft. In a small urban garden it can be kept to a more modest 3m/10ft. It looks splendid grown against a wall or over a pergola, with companions such as *Hedera colchica* 'Dentata Variegata' and *Humulus lupulus* 'Aureus'. Prune it in winter, cutting back lateral shoots to three buds from the main stem: it is vital not to delay pruning into the spring because the plant bleeds badly, and it will suffer a severe setback if it is cut once the sap begins rising.

DECIDUOUS CLIMBING SHRUBS, WITH AUTUMN FOLIAGE COLOUR
SUN OR SHADE   ZONES 5-9

VITIS VINIFERA

One of life's great pleasures is to pick and eat grapes fresh from your own vine – a treat rarely enjoyed by town gardeners. It is not a necessary deprivation. Many gardens have at least one sunny wall, and if you don't have a wall there are other possibilities: the vine I grew in a large pot on my London roof terrace was trained over a trellis arch around the glass door.

Among the cultivars that fruit best are 'Strawberry Grape' and 'Cascade' (also sold as 'Siebel 13.053') among the blacks and 'Chasselas Late' and 'Siegerrebe' for the whites. There are also some purely ornamental cultivars worth looking out for: the *teinturier* grape 'Purpurea' will not bear edible fruit, but it has attractive downy grey young leaves that develop to plum-coloured in summer and turn dark purple in the autumn. Another vine with striking foliage is 'Apiifolia' (or 'Laciniosa'), also known as the parsley vine, after its deeply dissected leaves. A newly planted vine will quickly establish a main frame of branches, growing some 90cm/36in. each season. Once these principal branches are established, the softer growth should be pruned hard back in winter to within one to three buds of the main stem.

DECIDUOUS CLIMBING SHRUBS, WITH AUTUMN FRUIT
SUN   ZONES 6-9

Vitis coignetiae, with *Hydrangea macrophylla*

PLANTS FOR BEDS AND CONTAINERS

AGAPANTHUS Headbourne Hybrids

Agapanthus, the flower (*anthos*) of love (*agapas*), comes from southern Africa, and is not reliably hardy in colder climates. The Headbourne Hybrids are the hardiest of the genus, but even these are best grown in tubs so that they can easily be moved indoors for the winter months. This effort is amply rewarded by the architectural beauty their presence brings to summer planting schemes. The deep blue to white flowers are clustered into large umbels that grow to 75cm/30in. tall and last from early summer through to autumn. The leaves are strap-shaped, with blunt, rounded ends, and arch in a distinctive way. Their delicate blooms look best among other flowers of pastel shades – pale pink and white begonias, nicotiana and lobelia – or, in a formal scheme, contrasted with evergreen topiary.

Agapanthus needs well-drained, moisture-retentive soil and a warm, sunny site. Plants do best facing the sun, as otherwise they tend to lean towards the light, particularly in a small, enclosed garden. The genus is related to the lily, and has similar thick, fleshy, slow-growing roots. They need plenty of feeding and watering during the growing season, but they flower best if slightly pot-bound. Once the roots reach the point of breaking the tub the plant can be transferred to a slightly larger container, or split and put into smaller ones.

You might also like to try the rather more tender *Agapanthus africanus*, which has more intense colouring and is ideal for cutting.
HERBACEOUS PERENNIALS, SUMMER FLOWERING
SUN   ZONES 8–10

ALCHEMILLA MOLLIS

Lady's mantle is the most accommodating of plants, growing on a dry site in sun as well as on a moist site in the shade. It associates well with most other plants, making a charming background for summer flowers such as lilies or campanulas, and a lovely underplanting for roses. The landscape gardener Lanning Roper used to edge borders with alternating alchemilla and catmint.

A herbaceous perennial, *Alchemilla mollis* dies right down in winter to emerge in the spring as a mass of tiny, roundish, frilly-edged leaves. The leaves are slightly cupped, and when they grow a little bigger rain and dew water collects at the base where the veins meet: it is said that alchemists' apprentices used to collect the pure water they needed for their potions from this source – hence the plant's Latin name. By the time the leaves reach their ultimate size of about 7–10cm/3–4in. across, they have flattened out.

The pale green flowers appear in early summer, spilling their frothy mass over the edge of the border or among surrounding plants. I like to use as many as possible in the informal flower arrangements I have in the kitchen throughout the summer, so I cut them regularly. Frequent cutting also encourages later crops of flowers, and minimizes the number of seedlings that appear all over the garden (once alchemilla is established it self-seeds very freely). Old plants benefit from splitting and replanting every few years, but otherwise this useful perennial needs only minimal attention.
HERBACEOUS PERENNIALS, SUMMER FLOWERING,
WITH ATTRACTIVE FOLIAGE
SUN OR SHADE   ZONES 3–8

BEGONIA

Begonias, though tender, are tolerant plants that are ideal for growing in containers, or for summer bedding. They thrive in sun or light shade, and flower from mid-summer until they are cut down by frost.

The flowers of *Begonia semperflorens* rise above the leaves in drooping clusters of white, pink or red petals. Its leaves are rounded and waxy, bright green in the white strains, paler green in the pink, and dark green with red tints in the red. The large-flowered tuberous begonias come in shades of yellow, pink, orange and red, and have slightly hairy green leaves, with serrated edges. Begonias look good in groups, but take care not to mix the pinks and the orangey-red

tints together, as they do rather clash.

At the end of the season begonias that have been planted in beds can be dug up and replaced by spring-flowering bulbs. If you pot up one or two they will continue to flower indoors throughout the winter.
HALF-HARDY ANNUALS OR HERBACEOUS
PERENNIALS, SUMMER FLOWERING
SUN OR LIGHT SHADE   ZONES 8–10

BRUNNERA MACROPHYLLA

I always like to have a good number of annual forget-me-nots (*Myosotis*) self-sowing with abandon around the garden. They look so pretty in the spring, creating a mass of pale blue from which my tulips and crown imperials emerge; they are also helpful in filling any gaps in the border. Of course,

A tuberous begonia in a pot
attached to an ivy-clad trellis

some will appear where they are not wanted, but it is easy to pull them out.

The perennial forget-me-not, *Brunnera macrophylla*, has similar blue flowers, typical of members of the borage family, but they are of a much more intense blue and carried on long stalks. The flowers appear in late spring, high above the leaves. Down at ground level the plant forms a neat mound of heart-shaped blue-green leaves that grow on after the flowers have faded. Several plants, spaced at intervals of 30–45cm/12–18in., make good ground cover in a shady position under trees. The variegated form, 'Dawson's White', is more attractive still, but needs plenty of moisture and shelter from bruising winds to prevent the silvery-white variegations from turning brown. Both look good with the yellow daisy-flowered *Doronicum* 'Miss Mason', fronting taller and later-flowering peonies.
HERBACEOUS PERENNIALS, SPRING FLOWERING, WITH ATTRACTIVE FOLIAGE
SHADE   ZONES 3-9

CAMPANULA POSCHARSKYANA
This campanula is often confused with the similar *Campanula portenschlagiana*. Both have difficult names to pronounce and I invariably end up referring to them as 'posh' and 'port'. Many people prefer 'port', for its rather more elegant appearance, but it requires more sun than 'posh', so 'posh' would be my first choice for the shady town garden. 'Posh' has the additional merit of flowering from early summer to mid-autumn, while the flowering period of 'port' is shorter.

The stems of both campanulas trail to about 30cm/12in. and both have shiny green heart-shaped leaves. The delicate flowers are bell-like and bright purple in 'port' and lavender-blue and more starry in 'posh'. Grow a single plant of either for a season and you will have quantities of flowers for summers to come, in every crack in the garden where seedlings are able to establish themselves. Yes, they are invasive, but it is easy enough to pull up any seedlings that you don't want, and you will be able to give them away to admiring (if unsuspecting) friends.
HERBACEOUS PERENNIALS, SUMMER FLOWERING
SUN OR SHADE   ZONES 3-9

CONVALLARIA MAJALIS
In France the tradition is to go into the woods on the first day of May to collect sprigs of lily of the valley, and then to offer them to relatives and friends as love tokens, or for good luck. France is, of course, blessed with an early spring: in less sunny climates it is rare to see lily of the valley in full flower until rather later.

The fragrant flowers of lily of the valley appear amid the clear green, elegantly elliptical leaves, first as tiny balls, then developing into the smallest waxy white bells. A large patch is arresting in appearance and in scent. They also look delightful intermingled with heucheras, tiarellas or forget-me-nots.

The plant spreads by means of thick, fleshy roots that should be planted flat about 2.5cm/1in. below the soil surface and no less than 15cm/6in. apart. It is more difficult to advise on position. Lily of the valley is an unpredictable plant and, in my experience, does not always thrive where one would expect. As its natural habitat is woodland, one might assume that it would like a shady spot under deciduous trees, but this is not necessarily so: in some soils and climates it does better in the sun. Your best chance of finding an area that has just the right ratio of light to available moisture is to plant roots in several different situations around the garden.

A mulch applied after the leaves have died down will help conserve the moisture that the roots need to build up the energy to grow again the following year.
PERENNIAL RHIZOMES, SPRING FLOWERING
SUN OR SHADE   ZONES 3-9

CROCUS CHRYSANTHUS
One year I planted up a cracked earthenware dish with about twenty-five corms of *Crocus chrysanthus* 'Cream Beauty' and left it out on my terrace for the winter. In very early spring, when I went out to inspect the garden, I found the crocus buds 15cm/6in. tall and on the brink of opening. I decided to bring them

Cyclamen hederifolium

into the kitchen where I could admire them in comfort. The effect of the kitchen's warmth seemed close to magical, as the pale creamy-yellow petals opened up all at once, revealing clear orange anthers. Since then I have never been without at least one pot of this hardy little crocus.

The species, which is rather smaller, with golden-yellow petals, can be found growing wild in Greece and Turkey, and all the varieties need well-drained, gritty soil and a sunny position. Those that flower early in the year will last longer out of doors if they are protected from frost and wind by a sheet of glass. Scores of cultivars are now available, and, as well as 'Cream Beauty', I particularly like 'Snow Bunting', which has cream petals with delicate purple feathering on the outside, and 'Zwanenburg Bronze', whose deep yellow blooms have a solid bronze mark on the outside of every alternate petal.
PERENNIAL BULBS, FLOWERING IN LATE WINTER AND EARLY SPRING
SUN   ZONES 5-9

CYCLAMEN HEDERIFOLIUM
It is often said that no garden can have too many cyclamen, and I am in complete agreement, for they flower in such profusion in autumn, a time of year when little else is in bloom. A few isolated cyclamen do not make much of a show, but they are obliging plants that will naturalize with ease in the shade of trees or walls, so that within two or three seasons you can have great carpets of autumn colour. Cyclamen are absolutely hardy, so long as they are planted in reasonably well-drained soil and are given an annual summer mulch of leafmould, peat or compost: this precaution is necessary because the tubers tend to rise up as they grow, so they are exposed to the risk of dehydration.

Cyclamen hederifolium (still sometimes called *C. neapolitanum*) is a native of the Mediterranean region. The flowers are about 1cm/½in. across and the reflexed petals, typical of the genus, look as if they were being blown back by the wind. They range in colour from mauve through pink to the white form, 'Album'. The flowers increase over a period of time and it is not unusual to see up to fifty slender stems on a mature corm. The grey-green, arrow-shaped leaves begin to

appear as the flowers fade, to remain throughout the winter. At the same time the flower stems curl up like springs, and eventually the seed is scattered freely from the pods. The seedlings need protection against mice, birds and slugs, so pot them up as soon as you see them and keep them in a cold frame until they are big enough to plant out once more.
PERENNIAL TUBERS, AUTUMN FLOWERING
SHADE   ZONES 6-9

DIGITALIS PURPUREA
The foxglove, a well-loved plant of woodland edges, is also delightful in the garden. Each plant consists of a flat rosette of leaves about 15cm/6in. across, from which the tall spire pushes up in late spring, reaching up to 1.2m/4ft in height. The tubular bell-shaped flowers have beautiful spotted internal markings that are worth examining closely – provided that a bee is not already collecting nectar deep within its throat, attracted by those same markings. *Digitalis purpurea* is a biennial, but once established it is easy to cultivate, as the plants seed themselves in late summer. You only need to sow seed in the first two years; after that, you can sit back and enjoy the progeny. In the wild, foxgloves grow in humus-rich leafmould, so it is a good idea to apply an autumn mulch.

Foxgloves vary greatly in colour: the species is a rosy red, and modern hybrids vary from purple through pale mauve-pink to creamy white and apricot. There is also a perennial foxglove, *D. grandiflora*, with yellow flowers. All look good in an informal planting, which might also include the blue-leaved, pink-flowered single rose *Rosa glauca* (*R. rubrifolia*), underplanted with feathery-leaved geraniums, or epimediums.
EVERGREEN BIENNIALS AND PERENNIALS, SUMMER FLOWERING
SUN OR SHADE   ZONES 4-9

ERANTHIS HYEMALIS
Beverley Nichols, author of *Down the Garden Path*, often wrote about how he could not bear to see the garden put to bed for a third of the year. He felt that it ought to carry on blossoming throughout the bleak, cold winter months: a dream at first, this became a reality as his gardening knowledge developed

and he became acquainted with the many plants that do bloom in winter. And of all the winter flowers *Eranthis hyemalis*, the winter aconite, was his favourite; he compared a winter garden full of these star-like flowers to a buttercup field in summer, for they have the same rich, oily yellow colour that shines so brilliantly against a frill of green bracts.

Aconites will even make a brave attempt to flower under ice, and they look their most charming peeping from a thin covering of snow. They are invaluable in a small garden, taking up little room yet making an impression out of all proportion to their size. They will spread happily among the stumps

In a box-edged border, tall mauve spires of *Digitalis purpurea* contrast in form, and harmonize in colour, with pale pink peonies.

Eranthis hyemalis

of dormant plants, tolerating the icy drips they receive from bigger neighbours, and benefiting from their shade in summer. This shade is essential to their well-being, since the tuberous roots will not thrive if they dry out. For this reason they should be planted in reasonably well-drained soil, under deciduous trees and shrubs, and in spring, while they are still green. Don't plant them in deep shade, though – they will open that much earlier in a spot that receives a little winter sunshine. I like a clump by the door, to greet me whenever I go out.
PERENNIAL TUBERS, WINTER FLOWERING
PARTIAL SUN OR SHADE   ZONES 4–9

EUPHORBIA POLYCHROMA

There is a euphorbia for every position, in sun or shade. *Euphorbia polychroma*, the cushion spurge, is among the most accommodating of them all, happy in either situation, so long as the soil is free-draining. This spurge is not only easy-going but also long-lived and reliable, pushing up its striking purple-green foliage and sulphur-yellow bracts just after the daffodils have faded. The bracts subsist into the summer and, as the autumn comes on, the leaves turn first green, then orange. It forms a neat mound about 30cm/12in. high, suitable for the front of the border, where it looks good in company with epimediums and the Cornelian cherry, *Cornus mas*.

Other worthwhile euphorbias include *E. griffithii* 'Fireglow', which has orange-red bracts and stems up to 75cm/30in. tall; and *Euphorbia myrsinites*, a prostrate form with grey-green leaves and bracts, which likes a sunbaked position and tolerates being stepped on, characteristics which make it ideal for a sunny street-side garden.
HERBACEOUS PERENNIALS, FLOWERING IN SPRING AND EARLY SUMMER, WITH ATTRACTIVE FOLIAGE
SUN OR SHADE   ZONES 4–10

FERNS

At the turn of the century, ferns – which had been so popular during the Victorian era – suffered from a change of fashion and declined into near obscurity. Luckily for those of us who garden in the shade, the wheel has nearly turned full circle, and nurseries are now offering an increasingly interesting collection of different species that are hardy and attractive. Many have beautiful, delicate foliage which unfurls in the spring, reaching maturity by the summer when they contrast well in texture and form with other foliage plants such as hostas, bergenias and Solomon's seal. Most have pinnate fronds that can be anything from 16cm/6in. to 1.2m/4ft in length. The smaller species, such as the tiny lady fern, *Athyrium filix-femina* 'Minutissimum', are suitable for edging a shady border; the larger ones, such as *Blechnum tabulare* and *Phyllitis scolopendrium*, give a light, airy atmosphere to the middle row of a border. There are also crinkle-leaved varieties, which are well worth looking out for in specialist nurseries. To succeed, hardy ferns require shade and a moist but light, well-drained soil, rich in organic content.
EVERGREEN AND HERBACEOUS PERENNIALS, WITH INTERESTING FOLIAGE
SHADE   ZONES 4–9

FUCHSIA

Fuchsias are far more versatile than many people realize. They are most often seen as accent plants in window boxes, tubs and hanging baskets, and indeed they are ideal for this role, but they also make beautifully coloured informal hedges, and they can be used as shrubs or bedding plants in a mixed border or rockery. However, although some of the hardier fuchsias, such as the species *Fuchsia magellanica*, can withstand frost, most are too tender to leave out during the winter; growing them in containers makes it easier to move them indoors.

Specialist fuchsia growers offer a huge range of different species and cultivars. All are showy – the writer Anne Scott-James compares them to dancers in Russian Ballet costumes – and they will flower continuously from early summer to the first frosts of autumn. I select among them with care, as I find some of the more garish combinations of tube and corolla colours rather overpowering, and they can clash with other plants. Among my favourites are 'Koralle', with salmon-pink flowers, 'Lena', with a pale pink tube and magenta corolla, and 'Swingtime', with scarlet tube and white corolla. 'Cascade', with its carmine tube and white corolla, looks good in hanging baskets.

Fuchsias should be grown in a well-drained, loamy compost and given plenty of water and nutrients during the season. Pinch out the leading buds to keep them bushy and to help restrict the height. Left alone, in the open ground, some varieties can grow to 1.5m/5ft, but those recommended for containers can be kept to around 35cm/15in. in height and spread.
DECIDUOUS SHRUBS, SUMMER FLOWERING
SUN OR LIGHT SHADE   ZONES 8–10

GALANTHUS

In my opinion every garden should have at least a few snowdrops to light up the winter months; and yet snowdrops are rarely seen in town gardens, despite the fact that they grow well in shady conditions.

I have heard people say that one snowdrop looks much like another, but the true galanthophile recognizes the special features that make each of the several varieties worth cherishing. It is fun to plant different ones: as

Pink and purple-red fuchsias stand out against a background of varied foliage, including, in pots, a dwarf fan palm and *Phormium cookianum* 'Tricolor'.

well as ensuring a longer succession of flowering, you will have the pleasure of observing the minutiae of detail in a little bunch picked to cheer the breakfast table. The common snowdrop, *Galanthus nivalis*, is one of the first in flower: there is always a single green spot on the inner petal of the flower. As well as the single-flowered species there are double forms, such as 'Flore Pleno'. There is also a cultivar with very short, broad outer petals, called 'S. Arnott'. *Galanthus elwesii* is a species with two green spots on its inner petals – these sometimes fuse so that the whole petal is green. Both species are scented and easy to grow in good, moist, well-drained soil.

Once a snowdrop colony is established the bulbs multiply well and can virtually be left to take care of themselves. If you do wish to move them, however, they should be split just after flowering, before the foliage dies back. Snowdrops look enchanting flowering among winter aconites, early crocus and Reticulata irises.

PERENNIAL BULBS, WINTER FLOWERING
SUN OR SHADE   ZONES 4–8

GERANIUM MACRORRHIZUM

Geranium macrorrhizum is one of the most reliable of the hardy geraniums; it thrives in both sun and shade and acts as good ground cover that thoroughly suppresses weeds but is itself never over-invasive. It grows best in a well-drained but moisture-retentive garden soil, but will tolerate drought, particularly in a shady situation.

As the name suggests, this geranium spreads by means of creeping rhizomes. It grows to 30–50cm/12–20in. tall. The leaves, which are 10–20cm/4–8in. wide with well-divided lobes, are pale green, turning red in the autumn, and pleasantly aromatic. Since its introduction in the sixteenth century all parts of the plant have been used for medicinal purposes and, to this day, the oil of geranium extracted from the leaves is an important ingredient of many scents. The flowers are about 2.5cm/1in. wide and in colour range from darkest magenta to delicate shades of pink. They open in early summer and will bloom continuously until early autumn; deadheading, with shears, to

remove the developing seedheads helps to encourage this repeat flowering.

The best cultivars are 'Bevan's Variety' (crimson-purple), 'Ingwersen's Variety' (pale pink) and 'Album' (white petals with a pink calyx). The evergreen leaves look good as a background to bulbs in the spring, and later in the season associate well with *Alchemilla mollis* and hostas.

SEMI-EVERGREEN PERENNIALS, SUMMER FLOWERING
SUN OR SHADE   ZONES 3–8

HEDERA HELIX

Ivies provide excellent ground cover for the shadiest corners of gardens; crocus, snowdrops and daffodils can grow through them in spring. They are also invaluable as background planting for winter, spring and summer window box arrangements, and for displays in pots and hanging baskets.

I once visited a small city garden where the owner grew a collection of a dozen different ivies in pots down the shadiest side of the house. The sight was splendid, and dispelled once and for all any notion that ivy might be a monotonous plant. The collection included variegated cultivars such as the silver 'Cavendishii', the boldly marked 'California Gold' and the silver and grey 'Glacier'; these were intermingled with cultivars with deeply divided leaves, such as 'Gavotte' and 'Königers Auselese' and crinkle-leaved ivies such as 'Big Deal' and 'Parsley Crested'. The owner made the collection even more interesting and attractive by encouraging some of the plants to climb up small pillars, while others were allowed to cascade over the sides of their pots.

EVERGREEN PERENNIALS
SUN OR SHADE   ZONES 4–9

HELLEBORUS

The Christmas and Lenten roses are among my favourite woodland flowers, for the pleasure they bring during their long flowering period and for the bold evergreen foliage that

In the moist position by a garden pool, variegated hostas thrive alongside a pale green maidenhair fern and the marbled leaves of *Saxifraga stolonifera*.

lasts throughout the year. The handsome divided leaves have a leathery texture and are usually a dark, shiny green that shows off the widely cupped five-petalled flowers to perfection. *Helleborus niger*, the Christmas rose, has pure creamy-white petals with yellow stamens, while the lenten rose, *H. orientalis*, varies in colour from palest green to deepest wine-red. A selection of differently coloured hellebores, planted together in a group, looks beautiful. I also like to see dark-flowered hybrids interplanted with pale yellow daffodils such as 'Lemon Beauty'.

I mulch hellebores thoroughly with leafmould in the autumn; this improves the drainage and water-retentive qualities of the soil, important factors in the successful cultivation of hellebores, particularly if they are growing in the sun.

EVERGREEN PERENNIALS, FLOWERING IN WINTER AND EARLY SPRING
SUN OR SHADE   ZONES 3–8

HOSTA

Hostas are among the most rewarding and versatile of those plants that are grown principally for their leaves. Miss Jekyll knew the worth of hostas (or funkias, as they were then called), and used them liberally in association with tree peonies, lilies, ferns, eryngiums and yuccas. Her famed skill in creating exciting colour combinations is well illustrated by her use of blue or variegated hosta foliage in these plant partnerships. More recently, both in the United States and in Britain, new hybrids have been developed, particularly by Paul Aden and Eric Smith, giving rise to numerous fine cultivars – too many to list here, but providing scope for growing a whole garden of hostas with no two plants the same.

The leaves of the hosta can be loosely described as lanceolate, but they vary from narrowly pointed leaves on long, graceful stems (as in *Hosta lancifolia*) to nearly heart-shaped ones with scarcely any visible stems (like those of *H. ventricosa*), and they range in colour from deep sea-green or blue (as in *H. × tardiana* 'Hadspen Blue') through much paler hues of blue-green (*H.* 'Krossa Regal') to solid yellowy greens (*H.* 'Royal Standard') and variegations of silver or gold in differing ratios (for example, *H. sieboldiana* 'Frances Williams' and *H.* 'Ginko Craig'). The green of the leaves is a useful guide to a hosta's preferred habitat: in general those with light green leaves and a high degree of variegation prefer sunny positions, while the dark-leaved varieties are happy in shade.

The lily-like flowers appear on long spikes in late summer; in some varieties, such as *H. plantaginea* and *H.* 'Honeybells', they are scented. They will be all the more abundant, and the foliage will be more lush, if copious quantities of organic matter are dug into the surrounding soil or applied as a mulch; hostas also like plenty of water in the growing season. Their only enemies are slugs, which tend to go for the weakly growing plants. It is a good idea to grow hostas in a raised bed, out of the slugs' reach.

HERBACEOUS PERENNIALS, SUMMER FLOWERING, WITH ATTRACTIVE FOLIAGE
SUN OR SHADE   ZONES 3–9

IMPATIENS

In recent years several good, strong strains of busy-lizzies (or impatience) have been developed, so that we can now grow out of doors what was once a tender plant suitable only for the greenhouse or conservatory. The new strains grow and flower as well in the difficult shady and cool positions in the garden as they do in the sunny spots. And many of them are dense and low-growing (to about 30cm/12in.), so are admirable for planting as edging, or in window boxes, hanging baskets or pots. Impatiens needs warmth and moisture to germinate, but at most garden centres you can buy plants ready for putting out as soon as the danger of frost has passed. Plant them about 20cm/8in. apart. They come in a variety of vibrant shades of shell pink, solid crimson, violet, luminous rose, salmon, orange, coral and pure white.

HALF-HARDY ANNUALS, SUMMER FLOWERING
SUN OR SHADE   ZONES 8–9

LILIUM AURATUM

Of all the lilies the Japanese golden-rayed lily has the widest flowers, with a diameter of up to 30cm/12in.; understandably, the plant caused quite a stir when it was first exhibited in London in the mid-nineteenth century. The purplish-green stems grow to 90cm/36in. or more and are clothed with narrow leaves up to 23cm/9in. long. The highly fragrant flowers are white with a yellow stripe down the centre of each tepal, which is gracefully curved back at the end, and speckled with maroon spots. In the centre are six filaments, each tipped with chocolate-coloured pollen.

Like most lilies, *Lilium auratum* needs a loamy soil with the addition of some coarse grit and peat or leafmould to provide sharp drainage and adequate moisture retention; it will not grow in alkaline soil. Plant bulbs 15cm/6in. deep. The flowers and stems need plenty of sunshine, but the bulbs should be kept cool and given liquid feeds throughout the growing season: this ensures that they ripen well and flower again the following year. I like to see a mass of flowers, so I always plant at least three bulbs together. Japanese lilies shine out against evergreen topiary or soft silvery foliage, and they are useful for filling gaps in the border.

PERENNIAL BULBS, SUMMER FLOWERING
SUN   ZONES 6-9

LOBELIA ERINUS

Although lobelias would scarcely be noticed if planted on their own, they make a strong support for many summer displays, especially in containers. There are two sorts of lobelia: compact forms look best massed amidst bedding plants to create a sea of blue; trailing lobelias are admirable cascading over walls, or the sides of hanging baskets or tall pots. Lobelias now come in many shades, from purple, mauve, and dark blue through to clear pale blue and even white. Begonias, fuchsias, pelargoniums, pot marigolds, petu-nias, alyssum, nemesias, ballota, *Helichrysum petiolare* – any of these would be happy choices for the main actors in the display.

Lobelia is a half-hardy perennial in warmer climates, but in cold climates it is usually raised from seed sown in the warmth in early spring, and planted out immediately after the last frosts. Raising them from seed yourself is the most economical way to produce a mass of plants; but in town it is often easier to buy them as seedlings from a garden centre.

HALF-HARDY ANNUALS OR PERENNIALS,
SUMMER FLOWERING
SUN OR LIGHT SHADE   ZONES 9-10

Impatiens, with *Oxalis articulata*, brings bright colour to a shaded courtyard.

MELIANTHUS MAJOR

'Sea green, pinnate, oily smooth; undoubtedly the most beautiful leaf in the whole border' – so the gardening writer Christopher Lloyd described this sculptural plant, which was introduced to the West from India as long ago as 1688. Except in the mildest climates, melianthus cannot be left to overwinter outdoors, as it gets cut down by frost, so it must be moved to a frost-free greenhouse or conservatory in winter; I would recommend growing it in a large tub, so that it can be moved easily.

Melianthus major grows to about 1.2m/4ft (if left unchecked to 3m/10ft or more) and has fierce-looking jagged-edged leaves that reach about 30cm/12in. in length. For a bold foliage effect plant it with *Hosta plantaginea* 'Grandiflora' and tightly clipped *Lonicera nitida* 'Baggesen's Gold'.

SEMI-EVERGREEN SUB-SHRUBS, WITH INTERESTING SUMMER FOLIAGE
SUN OR LIGHT SHADE   ZONES 8-10

MUSCARI ARMENIACUM

The grape hyacinth is now so common, and looks so much at home, in northern European countries and the United States, that it is hard not to think of it as a native plant; but, surprisingly, it was introduced, from Greece, as late as 1878. Grape hyacinths are not fussy and will grow in sun or shade, and in any type of soil. The bulbs multiply profusely, and once you have a few established they will quickly spread across the borders, under shrubs and among perennials. Their brilliant blue flowers, in tones from azure to purple, associate well with other spring-flowering bulbs such as late narcissi (for example, the white 'Thalia'), or lily-flowered tulips (such as yellow 'West Point' or pink 'China Pink'). And they look wonderful under a specimen tree such as *Magnolia stellata*, or in a lawn.

PERENNIAL BULBS, SPRING FLOWERING
SUN OR SHADE   ZONES 7-9

NARCISSUS

For me, spring would not be spring without a copious display of daffodils. They are jolly flowers, with their brightly coloured trumpets enveloped by a frilly perianth, and, as they herald the warmth to come, they withstand all but the worst of the spring weather.

The daffodil season starts early with some of the smallest cultivars. Among the first to flower are the charming cyclamineus hybrids: their name refers to the swept-back perianth segments. 'February Gold' (to 30cm/12in.) is a lovely bright yellow; Tête-à-Tête (15–20cm/6–8in.) often has two flowers on each stem, each with a pale yellow perianth and orange-yellow cup.

My favourite mid-season trumpet daffodil, 'Mount Hood', is tall (50cm/20in.), white all through and long-lasting. Next come the large-cupped cultivars such as 'Passionale', with a pure white perianth and soft pink cup. Finally another white cultivar, 'Thalia', closes the season: it has two, or even three, elegant, slightly drooping flowers per stem. All these daffodils can be planted in the open ground or in pots or window boxes. They will make a spectacular display with bright blue muscari and creeping ivy.

When your daffodils have finished flowering you should continue to water and feed them so that the bulbs can build up strength to produce flowers the following season. Ideally, the bulbs should be lifted at least every second summer, once the foliage has died back. Store them in a cool, dry spot and replant them in early autumn.

PERENNIAL BULBS, SPRING FLOWERING
SUN OR SHADE   ZONES 6-8

NICOTIANA ALATA

There are flowering tobacco plants in shades of purple, red, crimson, pink, palest yellow and green, and ivory white. They can be bought in packets of mixed colours or, increasingly, in single-colour packets, which I find more useful, as I like to grow specific colours to fit in with my colour schemes.

Nicotiana alata is usually 30–60cm/12–24in. high, but some plants grow as tall as 90cm/3ft. The pale green, sticky leaves cover the ground well. In a sunny position, the star-shaped, sweetly scented flowers open only as the sun goes down; in light shade they will open during the day as well as at dusk. If you want your plants to flower all summer long, it is best to sow the seed early, in the warmth; plant the seedlings out when there is no more fear of frost.

My favourite tobacco plant is the greenish-yellow 'Lime Green'. The flowers seem to glow in the summer evening light, and they look good either in a white display with *Lilium regale* and *Artemisia* 'Powis Castle' or with red plants such as *Penstemon* 'Schoenholzeri' and *Lobelia cardinalis*.

ANNUALS OR DECIDUOUS PERENNIALS, SUMMER FLOWERING
SUN   ZONES 8-10

OSTEOSPERMUM ECKLONIS

The South African daisy, or Cape marigold, has an electric quality that lights up a garden. The flowers have dark blue central discs and white petals that are tinged mauve on the underside: it is the clarity of the two colours, and the contrast between them, that makes the flowers so special. The plants grow in tight mats that spread quickly over the ground, or over the surface of a wide pot, and reach a height of about 30cm/12in. They look well growing among deep pink geraniums, border pinks and blue salvias.

South African daisies tend to keep growing fast into the autumn, and, still being full of sap, are particularly vulnerable to the first cold snaps of winter. So, to be on the safe side, move potted plants indoors for the winter, or, if your plants are in open ground, take a few cuttings in late summer.

Osteospermum is also often listed as *Dimorphotheca*.

EVERGREEN SUB-SHRUBS, SUMMER FLOWERING
SUN   ZONES 7-10

PACHYSANDRA TERMINALIS

Pachysandra, an excellent ground cover plant for shady areas, is unaccountably neglected in Britain, but it is used extensively in the United States, both in ambitious landscaping schemes and in private gardens. It is invaluable as an edging to a shady walk, under shrubs, in the shadiest courtyards or on steep slopes in half-sun or dense shade.

Pachysandra is 15–20cm/6–8in. tall and has shiny green foliage that quickly clothes the ground, excluding unwanted weeds. The variegated cultivar 'Variegata' is equally hardy and has leaves that never lose their narrow white margins. Plants should be put in at 10cm/4in. intervals in good, loamy soil that has been enriched with organic material such as peat, compost or leafmould. Initially the plants need to be kept well watered, but once established their dense foliage protects the soil from evaporation, and they virtually look after themselves.

EVERGREEN PERENNIALS
SUN OR SHADE   ZONES 4–8

PELARGONIUM

In many seed catalogues pelargoniums are still listed as geraniums, as that is the name they have gone under for as long as most people can remember. However, since the increase in popularity of the true geranium, the hardy crane's bill, pelargoniums are more frequently given their correct name.

All pelargoniums are tender plants, that in any but the mildest climate need to be under cover for the winter. Probably the hardiest, and best suited to outdoor use, are zonal pelargoniums, with their showy flowers and round leaves (often with a darkish mark – the 'zone' that gives them their name). Zonal pelargoniums were much favoured by nineteenth-century gardeners, who cultivated many interesting varieties that have, sadly, since disappeared. However, it was also at this time that the practice grew of bedding out serried ranks of bright red pelargoniums for instant effect – a custom that has formed and limited the common view of pelargoniums, although they come in white, many shades of pink, magenta and vermilion, as well as the vivid scarlet, and they look far better arranged in small groups. They are ideal plants for pots and window boxes.

Pelargoniums like a sharp-draining compost and need to be on the dry side, and slightly pot-bound, to flower successfully – if they are fed and watered too generously they tend to produce an overgrowth of lush green leaves at the expense of flowers. This does not mean that you should starve them completely, as they will not survive without some food and water, but there is an art to achieving the right degree of neglect. I must confess to a yearning for the wonderfully scraggy-looking plants that embellish window sills in Italian towns, crouched behind lines of washing, that display astonishing flowers.

Zonal pelargoniums are easily raised each autumn from seed, or bought in spring as small plants that can be put out after the last frosts. Alternatively, plants can be over-wintered indoors, on a sunny window sill, and cuttings taken in the spring; they will root easily, and grow on to provide plenty of flowers by the summer.

There are also geraniums that we value for their deliciously scented leaves rather than their flowers, which are usually insignificant. Of these my favourite is *Pelargonium tomentosum*, the peppermint-scented or flannel-leaved geranium. Both these common names describe the plant aptly, as the large grey-green leaves (up to 13cm/5in. long) are soft and velvety and smell strongly of peppermint when crushed. *Pelargonium tomentosum* has a sprawling habit and plants will grow vigorously to 1.2m/4ft in a single season. They make a marvellous display cascading over the sides of pots lined in tiers down either side of a flight of steps.

EVERGREEN SUB-SHRUBS, SUMMER FLOWERING
SUN OR LIGHT SHADE   ZONES 9–10

PETUNIA

There are vulgar petunias and there are distinguished petunias. The difference lies not in the plants themselves, but in the way they are used. In single colours petunias have style, but throw them together and they become a crowd of loud hooligans.

Petunias are perfect plants for filling summer gaps in the border and for growing in urns or vases. Provided that you are willing to spend time deadheading them regularly, they will give a good display from early summer through to the first frosts. The tiny seeds should be sown in early spring and the seedlings pricked on as soon as they are big enough to be handled. Plants raised this

A display of pelargoniums in shades of pink and mauve is set off by the pale grey foliage of *Helichrysum petiolare*, the black leaves of *Aeonium* 'Tête Noir' and the fleshy rosettes of *Echeveria glauca*.

Mauve petunias in a subdued flower arrangement

Pulmonaria saccharata, with hostas

way, or bought in late spring as seedlings, can be planted out as soon as the risk of frost has passed. Pinch out the tips to encourage bushy growth. Petunias need a sunny or lightly shaded position, and they should be kept on the dry side – but they will wilt if they are *too* dry. The Multiflora Resisto series and the Floribunda varieties both withstand drought, recovering quickly as soon as it rains; the large-flowered Grandiflora varieties need more frequent watering. Try a dark red cultivar with a small-leaved golden-variegated trailing ivy, a purple one with a South African daisy, or yellow and white ones with ballota.
HALF-HARDY ANNUALS, SUMMER FLOWERING
SUN OR LIGHT SHADE   ZONES 4-9

PULMONARIA SACCHARATA

One of the oldest of the many common names for pulmonarias is 'Joseph and Mary', for the two colours of funnel-shaped flowers – the young blooms pink, the older ones blue – that are simultaneously borne on one plant. For the same reason they are sometimes called 'soldiers and sailors'. And the spotty leaves have given rise to the name of 'spotted dog'.

The species *P. officinalis* is an old cottage-garden plant which was valued for its use as a poultice for chest infections (hence yet another name – 'lungwort'). It has been in cultivation since the sixteenth century. However, *P. saccharata*, introduced in the nineteenth century, is a plant with more presence. Its long, deep green elliptical leaves are heavily mottled with grey and covered with rough, hairy bristles, and do a splendid job of covering the ground so as to suppress all weeds. Plants should be put in about 25cm/10in. apart, in moist, fertile soil, preferably in shade; they look attractive among ferns and daffodils. Pulmonaria leaves occasionally become brown and untidy round the edges, and they should then be picked off: fresh ones will soon appear.
EVERGREEN PERENNIALS, SPRING FLOWERING
SHADE   ZONES 3-8

PRIMULA

Primroses (*Primula vulgaris*) and polyanthus (*P.* × *polyantha*) are a delight in spring, and they thrive in the cool conditions of a shady garden. For a simple, natural look, you can plant wild primroses with snowdrops under trees and shrubs. Alternatively, if you choose to investigate the many different strains and cultivars and broad range of colours – from red and pink to blue, gold and white – you will find that primulas can be chosen to complement any colour scheme. However, once they find an ideal spot primulas will tend to cross-pollinate and seed themselves unremittingly, so that you may well end up with a glorious carpet of different colours, which is what I have in my garden. I keep promising myself that I will be fierce and sort the colours out, but I always relent because they look so pretty in their unruliness.

Primulas can be raised from seed sown in the summer and planted out in autumn to flower the following spring; germination is erratic, however, and if you only want a few plants it is best to buy them in the autumn, for immediate planting out.
SEMI-EVERGREEN PERENNIALS, SPRING FLOWERING
SHADE   ZONES 4-8

RHODODENDRON Cilpinense

A cross between Himalayan *Rhododendron ciliatum* and Chinese *Rh. moupinense*, *Rh.* Cilpinense is one of the smallest rhododendrons, forming a rounded bush little more than 90cm/36in. high; so it is a good choice for growing in a container. The flowers are profuse, borne in clusters of three or five blooms, in varying shades of pink to white depending on the form. They are early and, although the plant is fairly hardy provided it is sheltered from cold, drying winds, the flowers need additional protection on frosty spring nights: just placing a net over the bush is sufficient to keep off the worst of the frost.

Like all ericaceous plants, *Rh.* Cilpinense needs acid soil or a peat-based compost, and plenty of nutrients throughout the summer. Prune as soon as it has finished flowering, taking care not to damage the new flower buds, which will already be forming in readiness for the following year. The roots need to be kept cool: with container-grown plants this can be achieved by burying the pot in the soil in a shady corner of the garden, once flowering is over. In cold areas it is wise to bring the plant indoors during the winter.
EVERGREEN SHRUBS, SPRING FLOWERING
LIGHT SHADE   ZONES 8-9

ROSMARINUS OFFICINALIS

Every time I brush past a rosemary bush I am delighted by the characteristic fragrance that instantly fills the air, even in the coldest months of the year. The rosemary's gaunt stems are covered with needle-like leaves that tend to point upward (this is especially so in the cultivar 'Miss Jessopp's Upright'). The flowers are small but by no means insignificant, since they cover the branches in spring and again in late summer. Darker forms, such as 'Benenden Blue' and 'Severn Sea', are attractive, but more tender than the species. It is sometimes possible to find white and pink forms.

Rosemary is happiest in a sunny position, in well-drained soil, and benefits from occasional feeding during the growing season. The crushed leaves of the herb have been used for centuries as a flavouring; rosemary is also the herb of remembrance, used by medieval apothecaries to comfort the brain and restore lost memory and speech.

EVERGREEN SUB-SHRUBS, WITH AROMATIC LEAVES
SUN OR LIGHT SHADE   ZONES 6–10

TULIPS

I have a great affection for tulips. Their proud flowers stand erect and bold in full sunshine, but I particularly like the way the stems turn and twist towards the light if conditions are a little shady, or if they are indoors in a vase.

There are charming dwarf species, such as the early-flowering yellow *Tulipa urumiensis* (10cm/4in.). Rather taller, at 30cm/12in., are *T. clusiana*, with white petals flushed crimson on the underside, and *T. fosteriana* (the white cultivar, 'Purissima', is especially lovely). Largest of all are the lily-flowered and the parrot-flowered tulips, and the double Darwin Hybrids, which all come in tints of white, pink, red, black, yellow and orange. Thousands of cultivars have been bred by specialist growers, offering a huge choice: make your selection with care. Some varieties have been in cultivation for centuries, and many of these would make a good choice for a garden in the style of a particular historical period. For example, 'Zomerschoon', dating from the early seventeenth century, with late single cream flowers streaked with salmon pink, might suit your garden. Or you could try the nineteenth-century 'Couleur Cardinal', an early-flowering single scarlet tulip with a purple tinge.

Species tulips can be left in the ground to flower for several years, but it is best to lift most other tulips after the leaves have died, and store them in a dry, airy spot before replanting them in the autumn into well-drained soil. Tulips look well with supporting plants such as forget-me-nots or wallflowers.

PERENNIAL BULBS, SPRING FLOWERING
SUN OR LIGHT SHADE   ZONES 5–9

VIOLA CORNUTA

The little tufted, or horned, violet and its hybrids make charming ground cover for a shady situation. They will flower for months, starting in late spring and lasting well into the autumn, provided that faded blooms are picked off and the plants are kept well watered. In shape the flowers are midway between the wild violet and the pansy: more substantial than the former and daintier than the latter. In colour they range from deep violet ('Lord Nelson'), through blue ('Belmont Blue'), to palest lilac (*lilacina*) and white (*alba*). They spread well, covering the ground with small velvety green leaves, and look especially attractive growing among hostas and lady's mantle.

EVERGREEN PERENNIALS, FLOWERING FROM LATE SPRING TO AUTUMN
SHADE   ZONES 5–9

VIOLA × WITTROCKIANA

Pansies are cheerful little plants that will brighten the front of any border, or bloom in a pot on a step or a narrow window sill, from late winter onwards. They come in all shades of red, yellow, blue, white and purple, with some fascinating bicolours.

Pansies are easily grown from seed and can be sown in early summer for flowering late the following winter, in autumn to flower in summer, or in early spring to provide blooms for autumn. They need a little feeding and watering in the winter, more during the summer, and require regular deadheading to prevent seed formation and encourage new flower growth.

HARDY ANNUALS OR BIENNIALS, FLOWERING ALL YEAR
SUN OR PARTIAL SHADE   ZONES 4–9

Tulipa urumiensis

Viola 'Belmont Blue'

SUGGESTED READING

Town and Small Gardens

Anson, Sir Edward R. *The Small Garden* George Bell & Sons, London, 1936

Field, Zenia *Town and Roof Gardens* Collins, London, 1967

Llewellyn, Roddy *Beautiful Backyards* Ward Lock, London, 1985; as *Little English Backyards* Salem House, Salem, 1985

Llewellyn, Roddy *Roddy Llewellyn's Town Gardens* Weidenfeld & Nicolson, London and New York, 1981

Loudon, John Claudius *The Suburban Gardener and Villa Companion* London, 1938; ed. John Hunt, Garland Publishers, New York, 1982

Roper, Lanning *Successful Town Gardening* Country Life, London, 1957

Seton, Lady F. E. *My Town Garden* Nisbet & Co, London, 1927

Sudell, Richard *The Town Garden* Ward Lock, London, 1930

Taylor, George M. *The Little Garden* Collins, London, 1948

General and Garden History

Dutton, Joan Parry *Plants of Colonial Williamsburg* Colonial Williamsburg Foundation, Virginia, 1979

Gibson, John and Weatherly, Neal *The Gardens of Williamsburg* Colonial Williamsburg Publications, Virginia, 1970

Hibberd, Shirley *Rustic Adornments for Homes of Taste* London, 1856

Jekyll, Gertrude *Children and Gardens* Country Life, London, and Charles Scribner's Sons, New York, 1908; Antique Collector's Club, Woodbridge, and Apollo, New York, 1982

Jellicoe, G. and S., Goode P. and Lancaster M. (eds.) *The Oxford Companion to Gardens* Oxford University Press, Oxford, 1986

Mumford, Lewis *The City in History* Secker & Warburg, New York, 1961; Penguin, Harmondsworth, 1973

Muthesius, Stefan *The English Terraced House* Yale University Press, New Haven and London, 1982

Stuart, David *Georgian Gardens* Robert Hale, London, 1979

Tunnard, Christopher *Gardens in the Modern Landscape* Architectural Press, London, 1938

Garden Design

Agar, Madeline *Garden Design* Sidgwick & Jackson, London, 1911

Bisgrove, Richard *Making the Most of your Garden* Ward Lock, London, 1976

Calkins, Carroll C. (ed.) *Great Gardens of America* Coward-McCann, New York, and Country Beautiful, Wisconsin, 1969

Church, Thomas D., Hall, Grace and Laurie, Michael *Gardens are for People* McGraw Hill, New York, (2nd ed.) 1976

Crowe, Sylvia *Garden Design* Country Life, London, 1958; Hearthside, New York, 1959

Hicks, David *Garden Design* Routledge & Kegan Paul, London, and Methuen Inc., New York, 1982

Hobhouse, Penelope *Colour in your Garden* Collins, London, and Little, Brown, Boston, 1985

Mercer, F. A. *Gardens and Gardening* The Studio, London, and William Edwin Rudge, New York, 1932

Page, Russell *The Education of a Gardener* Collins, London, and Random House, New York, 1985

Sudell, Richard *Landscape Gardening* Ward Lock, London, 1953

Plants

Bailey, L. H. and E. Z. *Hortus Third* Macmillan, New York, (3rd ed.) 1976

Bean, W. G. *Trees and Shrubs Hardy in the British Isles* John Murray, London, (8th ed.) 1970 to 1988

Fletcher, H. L. V. *The Fragrant Garden* George Newnes, London, 1965

Frederick, William H., Jr *One Hundred Great Garden Plants* Alfred Knopf, New York, 1975

Grey-Wilson, C. and Matthews, V. *Gardening on Walls* Collins, London, 1983

Harper, Pamela and McGourty, Frederick *Perennials; How to Select, Grow and Enjoy* H.P. Books, Tucson, Arizona, 1985

Phillips, Roger and Rix, Martyn *The Bulb Book* Pan, London, and Mad River, Eureka, California, 1981

Phillips, Roger and Rix, Martyn *Roses* Pan, London, 1988

Phillips, Roger and Rix, Martyn *Shrubs* Pan, London, 1989

Royal Horticultural Society *Dictionary of Gardening* Clarendon Press, Oxford, (2nd ed.) 1956

Scott-James, Anne *The Best Plants for your Garden* Conran Octopus, London, 1988; as *Perfect Plants, Perfect Garden: 200 Most Rewarding Plants for Every Garden*, Summit Books, New York, 1988

Thomas, Graham Stuart *Perennial Garden Plants* Dent, London, (2nd ed.) 1982

Zone Ratings

The hardiness zone ratings given for each plant indicate the approximate minimum temperature a plant will tolerate in winter. However, this can only be a rough guide. The hardiness of a plant depends on a great many factors, including the depth of its roots, its water content at the onset of frost, the duration of cold weather, the force of the wind, and the length and heat of the preceding summer. Because of the effect of the heat from buildings, and the protective influence of walls, many town gardens have a microclimate that is relatively balmy, and it is often worth trying plants that would normally be considered tender for the area.

Approximate range of average annual minimum temperatures zone

1	below $-45°C/-50°F$
2	$-45°C/-50°F$ to $-40°C/-40°F$
3	$-40°C/-40°F$ to $-34°C/-30°F$
4	$-34°C/-30°F$ to $-29°C/-20°F$
5	$-29°C/-20°F$ to $-23°C/-10°F$
6	$-23°C/-10°F$ to $-18°C/0°F$
7	$-18°C/0°F$ to $-12°C/10°F$
8	$-12°C/10°F$ to $-7°C/20°F$
9	$-7°C/20°F$ to $-1°C/30°F$
10	$-1°C/30°F$ to $4°C/40°F$

INDEX

Numbers in italic indicate photographs

ACKNOWLEDGMENTS

Author's Acknowledgments
I am most grateful to the many kind garden owners who have given their valuable time to show me their gardens and to discuss with me their trials and tribulations, and their triumphs. Special thanks must go to those owners who have allowed us to feature their gardens in this book, and also to Bill Angliss, Kay Begg, Nancy, Lady Henley, Mary Home, Shirley Nicholson, Professor and Mrs John Nye, David Pamment, Philippa Stock and Anthea Sutherland.

I am indebted to Peter Thoday, Peter Barnes, Dr Brent Elliott, Stephen Scrivens, Robert Bell and Todd Longstaffe-Gown for their help in technical and historical research. Warm thanks also to Elspeth Napier and Catherine Brampton for compiling the index, to Susan Berry who first asked me to write the book, and to Frances Lincoln and her staff for their involvement, help and attention.

Publisher's Acknowledgments
The publishers would like to thank the following people for their help in producing this book: Tony Lord for his expert horticultural advice; Tim Foster for initial design work; Jillian Haines for design assistance; Katy Foskew for endless patient and cheerful clerical help; Mr Kent Brinkley, Mr Jim Garrett and Ms Catherine Grosfils for information on Colonial Williamsburg. We are most grateful to all the owners who have allowed us to feature their gardens, and who have been generous in giving information and advice. We owe special thanks to Lady Barbirolli, Mrs Ruth Barclay, Kay and Craig Begg, Gwen and John Burgee, Miss Lucy Gent, Niccolò Grassi, Mrs Mary Hawgood, John Hilton, Saxon Holt, Mr and Mrs David Jalving, Charles Jencks and Maggie Keswick, Mr and Mrs Allan Lee, Penelope and Marcus Linell, Jackie McColl, Mrs Nan McEvoy, Camille Muller, Piet Oudolf, Jenny and Richard Raworth, Graham Rust, Martin Summers, Richard Tan, André van Wassenhove, Mrs Emily Whaley.

Editor	Jo Christian
Art Editor	Louise Tucker
Editorial Director	Erica Hunningher
Art Director	Caroline Hillier
Picture Editor	Anne Fraser

Editorial contributors: Christopher Catling, Susan Conder, Penny David, Sarah Mitchell

Garden plans by Ian Bott
Plan on page 10 supplied by Colonial Williamsburg

Photographic Acknowledgments
Serge Bailhache 66 left, 67
Michael Boys 1, 82, 83
John Brookes 6
Geoff Dann FLL © 22 bottom, 37, 40 left, 45, 59 left, 62, 128
Karl Dietrich-Bühler 16, 55, 106, 107
Derek Fell 10, 76, 77, 78, 79 (left and right), 127
John Fielding 133, 161 top
Felice Frankel 38, 104, 105
Garden Picture Library – Ron Sutherland 23, 28 left, 32, 47 left, 60
Garden Picture Library – Ann Kelley 28 right
Jerry Harpur 7, 8, 9, 17 bottom, 27 (Victor Nelson), 35, 41, 51 (Gail Jenkins), 53 (Victor Nelson), 57 (Jocelyn Ritchie), 110, 111, 112, 113, 120 (left and right), 121, 125, 155, back jacket (Gail Jenkins)
Marijke Heuff 12 (Mr & Mrs van Rappard), 14, 18 bottom (Marijke Heuff), 25 (Mr & Mrs Berenschot), 42 (Mr & Mrs van Rappard), 50, 54 (Mr & Mrs Adriaanse), 59 right (Mr & Mrs Hummelen), 146 (Mr & Mrs Dekker-Fokker)
Saxon Holt 24 top, 34, 68, 69, 70, 71, 88, 89 (top and bottom), 98, 99
Jacqui Hurst FLL © 33, 56 (both Mr & Mrs Raworth), 72, 73, 74, 75 (left and right), 100, 101, 102, 103, 141 (Mr & Mrs Raworth)
Peter C. Jones 1988 © 17 top (Dawn Mello), 63, 122, 123, 124 (left and right), front jacket (all Gwen and John Burgee)
Lamontagne 66 right
Andrew Lawson 13, 20, 21, 40 right, 46, 90, 91, 92, 93, 129, 135, 136, 139, 143, 144, 150, 152, 154
Tom Leighton 49 (Roy Alderson)
Georges Lévêque 36 left (Mrs Adriaanse, Middelburg, Holland), 36 right (Mr Geense, Holland), 43, 44 (M. Coutarel, Tarascon, France), 84, 85
Marianne Majerus FLL © 29 top, 30, 39, 47 right, 52 right, 58, 64, 65, 114, 115
S & O Mathews Photography 126, 130, 131, 138, 140, 145, 148, 149, 153, 159 (Beth Chatto), 161 bottom
Mon Jardin & Ma Maison/Broussaud/Duronsoy 96, 97
Camille Muller 24 bottom
John Neubauer 48 right, 116, 117, 118, 119 (left and right)
Sheila Orme 22 top
Gary Rogers 26
Ianthe Ruthven 18 top, 29 bottom, 94 right, 157 (Harold Clarke/Dublin)
David Schilling 61 (Ryan Gainey), 156 (Ginger Epstein)
Dino Scrimali 3, 15, 48 left, 108 (left and right), 109
Ron Sutherland FLL © 19, 86 (left and right), 87
Margaret Turner/GaLP, 52 left, 94 left, 95
Elizabeth Whiting & Associates/Karl Dietrich Bühler 80 (left and right), 81, Jay Patrick 160 top
Steve Wooster 151, 160 bottom

Professional Garden Designers
Mackenzie Bell 155; Gilles Clément 84, 85; DCA Landscape Architects 48 right, 116, 117, 118, 119; Duane Paul Design Team 19, 28 left, 47 left, 60, 86, 87; Ryan Gainey 61; Albert Glucina 23; Isabelle Green 24 top; Perry Guillot 17 top; Bertil Hansson 16; Madame Ulrike Klages à Munich 96, 97; Arabella Lennox-Boyd 18 top; Camille Muller 24 bottom, 66, 67; Piet Oudolf 106, 107; H. Riede 50; Nagao Sakurai 88, 89; Richard Tan 110, 111, 112, 113; Thomasina Tarling 17 bottom; André van Wassenhove 80, 81; Klaud Wettergren 55; Josephine Zeitlin 104, 105.